THE BEST OF
SOUTHERN STEAM

THE BEST OF
SOUTHERN STEAM
THE FINAL DECADE

ALAN POSTLETHWAITE

SUTTON PUBLISHING

First published in 2000 by
Sutton Publishing Limited · Phoenix Mill
Thrupp · Stroud · Gloucestershire · GL5 2BU

British Library Cataloguing in Publication Data
A catalogue record for this book is available from the British Library.

ISBN 0-7509-2457-8

Endpapers: front: 'West Country' class Pacific No. 34092 *City of Wells* restarts from Paddock Wood with an excursion train of Bulleid stock. *Back*: The 'Wealden Rambler' approaches the Up platform at Sheffield Park, double-headed by SECR class P tank No. 27 and LSWR 'radial' tank No. 488.

Frontispiece (**Plate 1**): Spectacular steam effects can be achieved on cold winter mornings when the air is crisp and the sun is low. Standard 2–6–4 tank No. 80089 obliges with a fine plume of exhaust as it emerges from the tunnel south of Oxted with a set of Bulleid coaches. Strong side-light brings out the rich texture of grasses and ballast as well as a stately skyline of tall mixed woodland in silhouette.

To Marion, the love of my life

Typeset in 10/12 pt Palatino.
Typesetting and origination by
Sutton Publishing Limited.
Printed and bound in England
by J.H. Haynes & Co. Ltd, Sparkford.

Contents

Plate 2: A warm summer scene at Shawford, featuring the strong lines of rebuilt 'Merchant Navy' class SR Pacific No. 35015 *Rotterdam Lloyd*. It heads the Down 'Bournemouth Belle' of twelve flat-sided Pullman coaches plus a parcels van. An impressive train is a primary requirement of a good action picture. Other elements are a balanced composition and interesting 'other detail'. Here they are provided by a framework of a shallow cutting – full of trees, grasses and wild flowers with colourful SR signals on their tall lattice post – and a line of telegraph poles fading into the distant curve. Finally, there are two operational bonuses – a plume of white steam from the safety valve, and a friendly wave from the crewman who should be the fireman (right-hand side). Let us take a ride!

Introduction

The final decade of Southern steam was characterized by a great variety of motive power, spanning some seven decades of design and construction. While every class might have been photographed from platform ends, the result would have been a somewhat monotonous operational record with little artistic merit. By moving within and between stations, on the other hand, one could find thousands of different settings, making the pictures more attractive. By taking care with timing, focusing, framing and the inclusion of 'other detail', compositions of merit would emerge to stir the soul as well as being a much fuller historical record. The best photographic collections therefore comprise variety of subject matter, variety of setting and many artistic styles.

Between 1958 and 1967, the author visited most Southern stations and walked some 550 miles of line from Kent to Cornwall, taking over 2,300 photographs. Some were for technical and historical records, others had elements of artistry. The best of the latter are collated here by compositional theme, covering the territory of the former Southern Railway (SR, 1923–48). Post-nationalization takeovers of certain lines by BR Western Region are ignored. At the same time, full recognition is given to pre-Group (pre-1923) locomotives, rolling stock and fixed assets which gave excellent service into BR days. While such historic items could be re-painted, re-numbered and re-titled, their basic form and character survived, adding further variety to the BR railway scene.

H_2O is a most interesting and useful compound which man has exploited in solid, liquid and gaseous forms. As a pure gas, it is called steam. When mixed with air, it is called water vapour. As water vapour cools, it forms into small particles of water or ice. Such formations are called cloud, fog, mist or 'steam exhaust from engines'. When such particles are re-heated by the sun, they evaporate and become invisible. If cooled further, however, they precipitate into rain, sleet, snow, hail or 'dirty smuts from steam engines'. The fascination of the steam railway derives not only from combinations of boiler and machine (the 'steam locomotive'), but also from the intriguing visual effects of motion and steam exhaust. In the correct proportions and in the right settings, such steam effects can be beautiful and captivating – a wonder of man's creative genius.

This book is a celebration of steam at its best. While many of the illustrations have been seen in the author's previous three-part series *The Last Days of Steam on the Southern*, they are repeated here to a larger format and a high standard of reproduction. The captions too are fuller, concentrating upon three main themes: factual (the train and location); aesthetic (the composition); and that 'other railway detail' which is so often overlooked in publications devoted to steam locomotion. The page layout is designed to make the fullest use of the space available, omitting headers and page numbers.

The author had a lineside photographic permit. Whole days were spent tramping the lines, searching for 'magic' locations and waiting for trains. One could freeze in winter and bake in summer – a water bottle was essential in the duffel bag. Spring was a favourite season, with fairly long days, long shadows and cool air (creating long trails of steam). There were elements of fortune regarding sunniness, exhaust effects, the presence of people and train quality (vintage, rarity, cleanliness, smokebox-first, etc.). After taking hundreds of pictures, however, the luck evens out and one slowly builds a collection of fine compositions. Most trains would be photographed for the record, but extra time and trouble would be taken to find those special settings.

The author developed his own styles of composition, although he was probably influenced subliminally by other photographers and painters of the 1950s, notably C. Hamilton Ellis (p. viii: *References 1, 2, 6*) and George Heiron (*Reference 3*). Other fine railway photographers are represented in *Reference 5* (below). Two favourite railway artists are represented in *References 8 and 9* (below) although their pictures were not seen until much later. A common desire of these steam enthusiasts was to depict a full railway environment, not just the bare locomotive or train. Such settings might include people, signals and station furniture, or broader still with a view down the track and of the surrounding countryside or town. The 'train in the countryside' was a favourite theme of the author's, but not obsessively so. Foreground signals and trees are other favourites. An open mind is needed.

The chapter on people is a little different, mostly 'opportunist' pictures with little time for considered composition or precise camera settings. Like press photographers, one had to be constantly ready for such opportunities, with just seconds to spare before they moved on or changed expression. The people are mostly alongside engines, so that chapter also includes some locomotive detail. The Index at the rear lists 184 locomotives in 47 classes and sub-classes. Counting Fratton as LBSCR and Bere Alston lines as LSWR, the location spread (by pre-Group company) is as follows:

London, Chatham & Dover Railway *	LCDR	18
South Eastern Railway *	SER	39
Joint SER/ LBSCR (Oxted–East Croydon–Redhill)		12
London, Brighton & South Coast Railway	LBSCR	40
Isle of Wight companies		15
London & South Western Railway	LSWR	48
Somerset & Dorset (joint LSWR/ Midland Railway)	S&D	12
Total Number of Plates		184

* Merged in 1899 to become the South Eastern & Chatham Railway (SECR)

Much of the author's work was a race against time, as the Railway Modernization Plan was implemented in stages. The end of steam in Kent came in 1961, followed in the mid-1960s by the Redhill–Reading line, the whole of the LBSCR and most of the LSWR. The Isle of Wight and the Bournemouth main line were last outposts of Southern steam, yielding to electrification in 1967. During the short reign of Richard Beeching as BR Chairman, most rural branch lines were closed while secondary lines and the Exeter main line were dieselized, truncated and/or singled. At the same time, local goods yards were closed and freight traffic declined rapidly. After a century and a half of supremacy, 'King Steam' was rapidly dethroned and a whole way of life came to an end. It is the role of books, videos, museums and preserved lines to secure the place of the steam railway in the social and industrial history of Southern England.

References

1. Ellis, C. Hamilton, *The Trains We Loved*, George Allan & Unwin Ltd, 1947.
2. Ellis, C. Hamilton, *The Beauty Of Old Trains*, George Allan & Unwin Ltd, 1952.
3. Heiron, George, many cover pictures of *Model Railway News*, especially 1956–62.
4. Betjeman, John and Casson, Hugh, *The Illustrated Summoned by Bells*, John Murray, 1960.
5. Adams, John and Whitehouse, P.B., *Railway Picture Gallery*, Ian Allan Ltd, 1962.
6. Perry, George, *King Steam – Selected Railway Paintings and Drawings by C. Hamilton Ellis*, The Sunday Times Magazine publishers (limited edition), 1971.
7. Brück, Axel, *Practical Composition in Photography*, Focal Press Ltd, 1981.
8. *Don Breckon's Country Connections*, David & Charles, 1991.
9. Woods, Chris, *A Romance with Steam*, Waterfront Publications, 1993.

1. Signal Settings

Signals are interesting by virtue of their colours, shapes and dispositions – usually perched at the top of a slender post, sometimes singly but often in clusters of two or more. Signals in train pictures can be used either as 'auxiliaries' (in the middle- or background) or as bold foreground statements, often with the arm raised above the train and a post occupying a full side of the frame. They can add much 'character' to a composition, especially if they are old or complex. Signal-boxes and water-columns are also found alongside signals at platform ends. Some of each are included in this chapter.

Compositions with foreground features often require a compromise of focusing – perhaps with 'infinity' out of focus (*Plate 12*) – or with a foreground feature left deliberately unfocused as an 'impression' (e.g. the bushes in *Plate 5*). Foreground signals, however, demand sharpness. To maximize Depth of Field, a small aperture is required (large 'f' number). For correct exposure (Light Value), a small aperture demands a slow shutter speed. A train with lateral movement, however, requires a fast shutter speed (1/300 sec or faster), otherwise the train becomes blurred:

Lighting:	Full Sun	Bright	Bright	Bright
Light Value:	15	14	14	14
Shutter Speed (sec):	1/300	1/300	1/125	1/60
Aperture:	f8	f5.6	f11	f16
Depth of Field:	10ft–inf	14ft–inf (or 12ft–60ft)	8ft–inf	5ft–inf
Moving Train:	sharp	sharp	blurred	jelly

This table of examples is for the author's 35 mm Voitländer Vito 'B' camera which had Depth of Field markings as well as Light Values and a locking mechanism to change shutter speed and aperture simultaneously. The data are for the relatively slow Ilford FP3 film (125 ASA, later changed to 64 ASA) whose small grain size is generally imperceptible for book-size reproductions.

Another way to increase Depth of Field is to use a faster film, although the resultant prints may be grainy. *Plate 28* is an example of grainy sky using Ilford HP3 film (200 ASA). One final solution is to photograph the train when it is stationary (*Plate 11*) or when approaching nearly head-on so that lateral train movement is only a fraction of its forward speed (*Plate 16*). Working out the best solution can be great fun.

The author was unusual in using neither a range-finder nor an exposure meter, relying instead upon eye skills for quick assessment of both parameters. A tripod was helpful, aiding accurate estimation of distance and obviating any possibility of camera-shake. Until 1960, the author used a Ziess Ikon folding camera with 2¼ square negatives. Then he upgraded to the 35 mm Voitländer with its 'bright line' viewfinder which allowed an approaching train to be seen with both eyes open. Reflex cameras were around at that time – ideal for focusing but expensive. It was an era before automatic cameras. Auto-exposure these days is a great boon, but auto-focus is useless for creative use of Depth of Field. The best railway photographers later used the SLR (Single Lens Reflex) camera with a range of interchangeable lenses for zoom and wide-angle, offering even greater variety in composition possibilities.

Plate 5: For improved visibility on curves and over sidings, signal brackets can be 'handed' to one side. Horam's Up home bracket has an extended platform, reinforced with top stays and a lattice cantilever. Pictorial framing is completed by the bank of silver birch and unfocused greenery on the right. The SR bracket is elegant but ancillary here to the train – a clean-looking set of Maunsells bound for Tunbridge Wells West, headed by a 2–6–4 class 4MT tank. Although the standard BR tanks were regarded at the time as intruders (having displaced ageing pre-Group locos), in retrospect they are quite beautiful, bristling with plates, pipes and machinery. No. 80146 is fairly clean apart from one chemical smear from water and the discoloured cylinder block and exhaust pipe.

Plate 3 (*opposite, above*): Near Shepton Mallet, a warm shadow is cast by standard 2–10–0 class 9F No. 92233 heading a holiday train to Bournemouth. The 'distant' signal is power-operated, supplied under the tracks from its own mini-telegraph pole. The SR arm and rail-built post are used for framing, balanced by the right-hand tree, telegraph poles and the S&D double-arch road bridge. These huge Riddles locomotives have strong lines but can look ungainly close-up or without soft surroundings. The graceful cutting, teeming with flowers, mollifies the beast – so dirty and besmeared with boiler chemicals. Note the contrast of bullhead and flat-bottom tracks.

Plate 4 (*opposite, below*): Up-sun pictures, with their deep shadow and reflected light, can produce powerful, dramatic effects. Stop signals on the 'other line' bring a sense of solidity and security in composition, as do loading gauges and steep banks in silhouette. These effects are combined at Woldingham to portray a long Up freight train headed by Maunsell 2–6–4 class W tank No. 31919, itself a powerful-looking machine. The sun is particularly low, reflecting off the boiler and wagons through a trail of smoke and safety-valve steam. Note the texture of the yard trackwork, also the new concrete cable channels awaiting installation for power signalling.

Plate 6: When a train is moving away from the camera, one's eye is drawn along the line, conjuring up images of romantic destinations. Here at Ryde St John's Road, LSWR class O2 tank No. 27 *Merstone* is signalled to take the right-hand road to Newport and Cowes. The SR signal bracket was installed during the late 1920s, its two lower arms being

removed in summer for double-track working as far as Smallbrook junction. Framing is completed by the SECR signal-box and by the LBSCR brake-third coach whose handles, hand-rails, hinges, smoking signs, washing streaks and door vent hoods (plain and slatted) are distinct, being three-quarters up-sun.

Plate 7: At the country end of Redhill, these short rail-built posts carry SR corrugated starting signals together with shunting discs, track-circuit diamonds and three-way mechanically operated route indicators. They make an unusual frame for an SECR class N Mogul, backing into the loop platform where Tonbridge–Guildford trains would reverse with fresh locomotives. Note the clusters of signal wires rising through the platform end-ramp, also the cables (for signal lamps) strung between the posts. This is essentially a portrait of signals enhanced by steam – a pragmatic solution when low-level signals dominate the end of the station.

Plate 8 (*opposite, above*): High Halstow's Up distant signal was mechanically operated on a rail-built SR post. It adds foreground interest and frames this lovely old train to Allhallows. Push–pull set No. 737 comprises LSWR corridor coaches – a composite and a brake-third with an SR cab end. The up-sun aspect brings out detail of the coach sides, underframes and bogies, and adds visual strength to the signal assembly. The overall scene is somewhat stark, however, lacking sky colour and scenery. The signal and train are also close, with lateral train movement of some 30 mph. It was over-ambitious for reconciling Depth of Field with shutter speed, resulting in slight blurring seen on the right-hand cab-handle. It remains an interesting picture but not a prize-winner.

Plate 9 (*opposite, below*): Signals and winter trees frame an SECR push–pull train on the Down approach to Hurst Green. The low sun creates a mottled effect of shadow across the tracks. A sense of movement is created by the puff of re-starting steam and the half-raised 'distant' signal. This SR signal arrangement is unusual, with separate low-level posts for the twin distant arms, no doubt a cheaper solution than a bracket. Push–pull set No. 659 is signalled to take the direct line to Tunbridge Wells West via Hever. The SR cab end is similar to that on the LSWR coach in *Plate 8*, but the SECR coach is narrower, making the low elliptical roof profile appear less flat. Both trains are propelled by an SECR class H tank, but this North Downs setting is the more satisfying.

Plate 10: Long, straight elevated lines can be difficult to photograph. Failing an elevated viewpoint, one can use sky colour, signals and other lineside features. Worgret junction's 'distant' signal is used here, together with a small mile-post, blue sky and white cirrocumulus. LSWR class M7 tank No. 30056 heads a train to Swanage.

Plate 11 (*opposite*): A bold use of Slinfold's starting signal to frame SECR class H tank No. 31322, heading a push–pull train of Wainwright and Maunsell stock to Guildford. The SR arm is corrugated. The LBSCR post is tapered, of square section, and painted white. The summer scene is enhanced by full-leaf trees, a grassy bank and the white-painted station building. Depth of Field was no great problem, since the train was stationary.

Plate 14: A majestic signal bracket in a deep, shallow-angled cutting at Groombridge junction (these days part of the preserved Spa Valley Railway). The platform is greatly cantilevered for better visibility on the curve, reinforced (above, below and to the right) to take the bending forces due to the weight of three arms, ladders, dolls and maintenance men. The train to Tunbridge Wells West is interesting but subsidiary – a push–pull Maunsell set propelled by class H tank No. 31551. The setting is rich with silver birch, shrubs, wild flowers and grasses, enhanced by a fogman's hut and a distant overbridge. Fogmen were trained at London Bridge and could be drawn from all grades – trackmen, yardmen, signalmen, stationmen and office workers. Their unenviable job in the clammy coldness was to apply and remove detonators according to the signal positions. For electrified lines, they also had a thick rubber mat. The logistics of assembling such a hardy army quickly were formidable.

Plate 12 (*opposite, above*): At the start of rural Surrey, raised semaphores at Selsdon offer a farewell salute to a steam train speeding towards Sanderstead. They take the mind's eye to possible south-coast destinations like Eastbourne and Lewes, but the electrified Mid-Kent line (left) is a reminder that this is also commuter-land to London. The scene lacks sunshine, but interest and framing are provided by the Saxby & Farmer signal-box, unfocused signals and telegraph poles (left), also the foreground safety railing, SR concrete ballast bin and a fogman's hut. Note that one signal arm is flat, the other corrugated, precluding possible transposition. The rear carriage is SECR 'Continental' stock – with rear windows and flat, narrow sides (in contrast to the Maunsells beyond).

Plate 13 (*opposite, below*): During the late 1950s, LBSCR class K Mogul was arguably the loveliest of locomotives to be found in regular service along the south coast. The curved spectacles, flared running plate and low tender are in perfect harmony. No. 32337 is seen at Fareham, blowing off steam and heading a long mixed freight coming off the Eastleigh line. It is framed by a wealth of railway interest – signals, lamps, signs, a water-column, ballast bin, assorted wagons and a man working on a shunting disc. Two methods of signalling are seen at this three-way junction: a lattice bracket (left) with individual starting semaphores; and (right) an SR rail-mounted single semaphore with an electric route indicator. But our eyes always return to Lawson Billinton's handsome engine.

Plate 15: By Hove marshalling yard, a composition of signalling – clear but stark because of the absence of sky colour. SECR class N Mogul No. 31411 is framed, indeed overpowered, by the main feature: an SR balanced bracket with an unusual array of mechanical and colour-light signals, with a starting arm, 'distant' lights and a ringed arm for 'entry into sidings'. The Saxby & Farmer signal-box has lost its locking room windows but has been extended, presumably for power signalling equipment. Note the tall yard lamp, wooden hut and concrete coal bin.

Plate 16 (*opposite*): A bold, challenging signal composition with Oxted's outer home, requiring a Depth of Field from about 10 ft to infinity. A fast train approaches, but not too near and almost head-on. Low winter side-light brings out the grass texture and all the mechanical detail of the SR signal, its lattice post and steadying guy. Beyond the range of wire operation, an electric motor box is located beneath the balance arm. To the right are a terminal box and a fogman's hut. Everything frames SR class U1 Mogul No. 31907, making steam to Victoria.

Plate 17: By definition, a signal *bracket* is a platform with a single support column whereas a *gantry* spans the tracks with supports on either side. When combined with semaphore signals, gantries can be imposing, sometimes resembling a cathedral organ. On the approach to Worting junction, a tall girder gantry frames a train of Bulleid stock from Exeter headed by 'Merchant Navy' class Pacific No. 35001 *Channel Packet*, first of its class. All five arms are electrically operated – the raised ones are for the Southampton line. Although lacking finials and any other ornamentation, the signalling vies with the train as the focus of attention, almost winning! Additional framing and interest are provided by the row of great telegraph poles, the terminal box (bottom left) and the concrete platelayers' hut. Apart from 'rebuilt' characteristics of the locomotive, the scene is pure SR.

Channel Packet was a war machine of 1941,
From Bulleid's 'Merchant Navy' fleet, Pacific number One;
In air-smoothed form, it served in Kent and bore the 'Golden Arrow',
But when rebuilt, it lost its cloak and ploughed a different furrow;
Westward-bound with Walschaert's gear and standard lubrication,
Through Salisbury to Exeter with fast reciprocation.

(Author)

Plate 18 *(top)*: Colour-light signals are less photogenic than semaphores and can look incongruous with steam. At the London end of East Croydon, BR colour-lights of 1953 vintage are nevertheless used as ancillaries to frame an approaching through-service headed by 'West Country' class Pacific No. 34003 *Plymouth*. (The precise service is uncertain.) Supporting a four-aspect cluster, the simple right-hand post contrasts with the long, graceful cantilevered bracket on the left. Note the modern brick signal-box, the lone passenger on the left and the double-slip pointwork on the right. Our eyes return to the locomotive, however, with its drifting smoke and the half-face of a driver. Strong side-light emphasizes all the nooks and crannies of this rebuilt, imposing power-machine.

Plate 19 *(bottom)*: When Oxted steam trains passed each other at East Croydon, there was a curious arrangement of right-hand running. From platform 6 (right), the eastern-most running line was bi-directional (as far as the junction at South Croydon). When two such trains were photographed at the London end, it was important that the approaching locomotive was not too close, otherwise the station environment would have been lost. The immaculate Bulleid coach (right) is balanced by an open scene to the left, revealing the signal-box, several signals, gas lamps and passengers as framework. Compared with *Plate 18*, the colour-light post is now a central feature – interesting but still ancillary. It is the fine locomotive which again captures our attention, the various protuberances of Fairburn 2–6–4 tank No. 42090 standing out intriguingly in the low morning side-light.

Plate 20: Nanstallon halt was unmanned except for the signalman/crossing-keeper. His picturesque LSWR signal-box housed a ground-frame and sported a brick chimney. Here it frames a train from Bodmin General, re-starting towards Wadebridge behind an unidentified GWR Prairie tank. Framing is completed by the level-crossing, telegraph pole, a backdrop of trees and light cumulus. Little steam is visible on this summer's evening, but the scene is rich in texture due to the warm, low side-lighting. It is a scene of tranquillity, not of action. Note the two timber tunnels to protect wires and rods. The role of the up-turned dining chair is less certain.

Plate 21 (*opposite*): Lewes was complicated, like a double-slip point with a station in the vee at one end and a freight yard at the other. The throat was guarded by the Saxby & Farmer signal-box and by a forest of SR signals on lattice brackets at the ends of four platforms. In this study, there are eight starting arms plus four with an 'S' for 'entry into sidings'. Although numerous, the signals are ancillary to the central feature of composition – an inverted U-shaped LBSCR water crane in semi-silhouette. Using a tripod and much care for Depth of Field, a sequence of six pictures was taken. This one has a mixed freight train approaching, headed by Maunsell 0–6–0 class Q No. 30533. Note also the second crane, an LBSCR fluted lamp standard, SR enamelled signs, a flower tub, sky colour and distant quarries. It is a complex composition, made to look simple.

Plate 24: Salisbury is a busy junction station with four through-platforms, two bays and a mass of sidings. The Down 'Atlantic Coast Express' draws slowly into platform 4 headed by rebuilt 'Merchant Navy' class Pacific No. 35014 *Nederland Line*. Framed by the LSWR signal bracket, tall lamp standards and the great platform canopies, the scene is brought to life by railwaymen and waiting passengers. Signalled for the Westbury line is a Western Region diesel-hydraulic Hymek. The semaphores are electro-pneumatic. The camera is mechanical.

Plate 22 (*opposite, above*): The Down starting signals at Paddock Wood were mounted on an SR cantilevered gantry. Because of bridge obscuration, the through line had co-acting arms on two tall dolls, braced in three directions using auxiliary support posts. Framed centre-left is an immaculate excursion train of Bulleid stock headed by light Pacific No. 34092 *City of Wells*. Re-starting with a puff of smoke, it is about to take the curve towards Maidstone West. To the right are a three-way trailing point, a small silhouette of platform canopy and the grimy SER wooden signal-box. This box spans the start of the Hawkhurst branch and offers an enticing view along the dead-straight main line towards Folkestone. This is a balanced composition which can be perused for ages.

Plate 23 (*opposite, below*): At Brixton junction, the elevated LCDR main line is threaded miraculously between modern department stores. Victorian splendour is provided by the turret on the right and by the unique LCDR signal-box, perched above the tracks and advertising yet another store. It is a fine town setting for SR 2–6–4 class W tank No. 31912, taking a heavy freight on to the Catford Loop with just a wisp of steam. Using lamps instead of the usual Southern discs, the headcode announces the destination to be Hither Green yard (reached via Lewisham). The armless dolls on the signal gantry date the picture to 1959 and tell us that the signal-box is closed.

Plate 25: This tall LBSCR signal near Horam is an ideal frame for standard 2–6–4 tank No. 80014, heading an Up train of flat-sided Maunsells. The fixed-distant arm and its post are tapered. There are three guys, one via a shorter square post with finial. Both posts are reinforced with old bullhead rail, but who dares climb the ladder?

2. Telegraph Poles and Huts

The electric telegraph was developed for the railway in 1837 by William Cooke and Charles Wheatstone. After trials on the London & Birmingham line, it was first installed commercially on the Great Western, using cables at track level, soon followed by other railways. Overhead wiring was introduced during the 1840s, and wooden poles became a standard, familiar feature of the steam railway. They could be used for compositional framing as visual stops (singly) or as pointers (in a line) to draw the eye along a particular route. In pairs (to either side of the tracks), an 'echo effect' could be created, always pleasing to the eye. Sometimes they got in the way of train photography. They could seldom be ignored, demanding careful camera positioning.

Telegraph lines served several purposes, all carrying electricity. The primary railway role was to facilitate instant communication between signal-boxes using bell codes, miniature position indicators and telephones. Many devices used an earth return, so a single copper wire usually sufficed per circuit. Further railway uses evolved with the development of electrical appliances, including signal lamps (replacing oil) and motor-operation of remote signals and points (which might require a hand-cranked generator in the signal-box). To avoid interference with communication signals, the heavier electric circuits generally used pairs of wires rather than an earth return.

An early additional role of the telegraph was the transmission of Greenwich Mean Time throughout the world. Hourly signals were transmitted from the Royal Observatory at Greenwich, originally via the SER at Lewisham. It was the GWR which had first identified the need for standardized railway time – Bristol, for example, had been some 15 minutes behind London using local times, causing confusion in train scheduling. As the telegraph system grew, trunk routes (both road and rail) were rented out for public, private and government lines. Strategic towns like Portsmouth would have been early targets for Admiralty connections. Clapham cutting (LSWR) provides a prime example of the massive overhead telegraph, carrying some 120 wires on three sets of poles (*Plate 32*). Only a fraction of these would have been for railway use.

With the end of steam, the overhead trunk telegraph was superseded by multicore cables, now largely superseded by fibre-optic cables. (Wooden poles are still used for local phone lines, especially in rural areas.) The railways widely adopted multicore cables laid in concrete channels from remote, central control centres. These days, high-frequency control signals can be superimposed upon high-voltage electrification cables and in the running rails. Radio is used increasingly for direct links with train crews. None of this is photogenic or obvious, except for concrete channelling.

Platelayers' huts are highly photogenic. Their use is twofold – for storage and shelter. Detonators, flags, lamps, oils, scythes, sickles, forks, shovels, hammers, picks, spanners, keys, etc. would be stored there. Huts generally had a well-maintained, well-used sooty chimney. Loco coal was too anthracitic for open grates, so a mix of coke and wood was burnt, including chopped-up old sleepers. A linesman would be detailed an hour or two in advance of the lunch-break to light the fire and to put the kettle on. In the depths of winter, the fire would be lit first thing in the morning. In bad weather, most of the working day could be spent in the hut. One can only speculate upon the tales that were told while enjoying bacon, hot pies and tea made with condensed milk.

Plate 26: On the LCDR main line a few miles west of Faversham, a single telegraph pole is put to good effect about 25 ft from the camera. It is the solid reference point for full framing of an Up boat train of Thanet stock, headed by light Pacific No. 34101 *Hartland* – coasting with the regulator shut, laying a light trail of smoke. The frame is completed by the cutting and bushes (right), foreground grasses and an overhang of oak leaves, not forgetting the distant overbridge. The train side is in shadow but reflects the sky, particularly from the flat-sided Maunsell coaches. The sun picks up the front of the engine nicely, the focus of our attention:

> The hundred and first year of steam on the East Kent line will reveal
> The hundred and first Light Pacific – a hundred and more tons of steel.
>
> (*Author*)

Plate 28 (*opposite, below*): At Weald Intermediate (between Tonbridge and Sevenoaks), this full composition uses telegraph wires and cable, the 'echo effect' of two poles, and a 'train emerging' effect from behind the SER wooden signal-box. Tall grasses and sky colour complete the framing of 'Battle of Britain' class Pacific No. 34078 *222 Squadron* on a fast train to Charing Cross. Shot with a fast film, the streaky cirrus is somewhat grainy but creates an oil-painting effect which is quite acceptable in this instance. One can readily imagine the Lincolnshire Spitfires of 222 Squadron which fought hereabouts in the summer of 1940. Regarding the debate of Pacific good-looks before and after rebuilding, the jury is still out! Either version is attractive

Plate 27: In a wide cutting on the SER main line near Smeeth, the Up 'Golden Arrow' makes a grand sight behind an immaculate rebuilt 'West Country' class Pacific No. 34100 *Appledore*. Diffused sunlight reflects beautifully from the smokebox, deflector, boiler barrel and firebox. This 'operational record' becomes a 'composition of merit' by the inclusion of telegraph poles, a lone tree, and a platelayers' hut – our reference point, semi-camouflaged in undergrowth. Note the 'echo effect' of the two telegraph poles – what messages do they carry?

Plate 29: In a fairly featureless shallow cutting near Wye, the right-hand trees and a tractor were used as a visual stop, but the telegraph intruded from any elevated position on the lighter near-side. This bold, off-beat solution makes the nearest pole the centre of composition, bisecting the train. It seems to work, although the picture is rather spoilt by the locomotive – dirty and running bunker-first. Standard 2–6–4 tank No. 80034 heads a clean set of Maunsells with a four-wheel utility van at either end. The picture is 'softened' by the rich texture of the foreground grasses and by the long trail of steam exhaust, standing out against the overlay of thin cloud.

Plate 31: On Purley Downs near Sanderstead, a shot of pure power featuring standard 2–6–4 tank No. 80141. Taken almost up-sun using the tripod and a hand-held trigger, a low camera position was selected and shaded to bring out: (a) the train emerging from bushes, leaning into the curve; (b) low morning sunlight reflected from the train, picking out the multiple billows of steam and making the foreground grass glisten; (c) a full framework of winter trees and bushes, topped by a lone telegraph pole standing sentinel – our visual stop and reference point. Much of the locomotive is in deep shadow but this is an impressionist portrait, not a technical record. Such close-ups at speed are rare, requiring perfect timing for the train position. The square frame adds to the power.

Plate 30 (*opposite, below*): A pleasant country scene south of Mayfield, featuring standard 2–6–4 tank No. 80153 (clean but not gleaming) and its half-leaning driver. The train is framed by a pair of telegraph poles, leaning into the curve, together with their wires and a row of concrete fence posts. Note the glorious cloud colour, with half the frame filled with rolling shades of grey and white 'overcast'. Interest focuses upon the train, a wondrous combination of designs spanning some forty-five years of construction history. The BR locomotive is post-war, the SR utility van and rear corridor set are from the inter-war years, while the non-corridor set is LBSCR, *c.* 1910, to which an SR push–pull cab-end has been added to the brake-composite. Note the up-bowing of the second coach.

Plate 32: In Clapham cutting, a dramatic study of great telegraph poles, enhanced by trains and a long skew bridge of brick arches and a central steel beam. Heavy SR Pacific No. 35012 *United States Line* heads a Down express of mixed SR stock. Note the guys, wires, trees, sky colour and distant poles with multiple 'echo effects'.

Plate 33: A pastoral scene at the less bleak end of the Hoo peninsula. SECR 0–4–4 class H tank No. 31193 heads an Up train of Maunsell stock between High Halstow and Cliffe. The pagoda roof and protuberances – dome, chimney and pumps (for push–pull controls and brakes) – stand out clearly in this shot into diffused sunlight. Using the telegraph pole as a visual stop and reference point, framing is completed by the farm crossing, dark bushes (right), soft strands of foreground grass, a distant ridge (left) and bands of cloud-cover in grey-white.

Plate 34: In contrast to the two spars and six insulators near High Halstow (*Plate 33*) this trunk telegraph pole at Shawford carries twelve spars and about sixty insulators, resembling a flock of autumn starlings. It provides the sturdiest of visual stops, balanced by the larger but softer goods yard on the right with its mellow LSWR goods shed, a bank of trees, the approach road, a double-slip point, twin levers, concrete ballast bin and a loading gauge over the grass-infested sidings. They frame rebuilt 'Merchant Navy' class Pacific No. 35030 *Elder Dempster Line* on an Up Bournemouth express of mixed BR/Maunsell/Bulleid stock. It is the disused goods yard, however, that captures our hearts and minds. Note the weather-boarding, glazing and canopies of the shed.

Plate 35: A classic country branch line scene at Ashurst, featuring SECR class H tank No. 31005 with a Maunsell push–pull set. Taken from a low camera position, three-quarters up-sun with a half-yellow filter, the vigorous ostrich-plume of exhaust steam stands out with 3-D effect against the underside of cumulus. There is gentle, all-round framing from trees, bushes, grasses, the distant station and raised signal. They create narrow triangles with the train and track, tapering to infinity beneath the footbridge. Key reference points and visual stops are the dark outlines of the telegraph pole and platelayers' hut, the latter complete with rolls of fencing wire. Although the composition is two-thirds 'skyscape', we focus upon the train, the stately exhaust plume and the quintessential Edwardian outline of the locomotive. The scene offers a suitable transition to the next chapter, since the train is crossing the steel bridge of the River Medway, the boundary thereabouts of Kent and Surrey.

3. Bridges and Tunnels

Tunnels and bridges over the railway provide a wealth of framing opportunities for photography, either in the middleground as a principal feature or as a more distant 'visual stop', perhaps at the base of a hill. When a train is caught entering or leaving a tunnel, we are left in awe of the audacity of its crew and passengers. The swirl of sulphurous smoke and steam at a tunnel mouth can add a feeling of satanic menace and foreboding. Who dares enter here? – not I! The hill behind the tunnel can also be formidable and beautiful, often covered in trees and rich undergrowth.

By standing beneath a platform bridge, a silhouetted frame can be created of graceful shape and with textured masonry. Most bridges and portals have interesting design features, some with architectural merit. All capture our imagination, recalling the challenges that must have confronted the company when planning, financing and building the line. Examples in this chapter show the use of brick, stone, concrete and steel in bridge construction. All the tunnel portals are brick.

Bridges under the railway are less common in photography. The main exceptions are rivers (if the banks are readily accessible) and wide valleys which are crossed by viaduct. A common definition of a viaduct is a bridge of five or more arches. Everyday language is flexible, however, belonging to the people rather than to purists. We therefore find such misnomers as Holborn Viaduct and London Bridge which, strictly speaking, should be Holborn Bridge and London Viaduct. But not to worry!

Deep cuttings can be found on tunnel approaches, offering elevated viewpoints which are ideal for train photography. Cuttings may be steep-angled (e.g. through chalk or greensand) or shallow-angled (e.g. through clay, liable to slip). Examples of each can be seen at opposite ends of Sevenoaks Tunnel (*Plates 118* and *125*). The thickness of tunnel linings and the strength of tunnel portals reflect the stability, permeability and height of the ground. A head of ground-water must be held back. Compare, for example, the massive portal of Penge (*Plate 58*) with the much lighter ones near Heathfield and Rotherfield (*Plates 56* and *57*). The clay spoil from Penge Tunnel was used to bake bricks for its own lining, an early example of recycling. The Southern had many tunnels through chalk, sandstone and greensand, but none through very hard rocks like granite. There are therefore no unlined tunnels or unportalled entrances.

Victorian tunnels and cuttings were dug mainly with the pick and shovel, aided by barrows, wagons, horses and perhaps a steam locomotive. The spoil which was dug was used to build embankments, some of which required oak piling to achieve stability. On a perfectly surveyed line, the total volume of spoil was an exact match of embankment requirements, mile by mile. This gave optimum productivity in construction. In undulating country, we therefore find frequent transitions between cuttings and embankments, and these can be most photogenic (*Plates 117, 167*).

Embankments, on the other hand, can be difficult for railway photography, often resulting in the camera being too close to the train or tilted up from below with distortion and sky-glare. One solution is to photograph the train nearly head-on, using a signal for added interest (*Plate 10*). Another solution is to gain elevation on lineside features, with due regard for safety (*Plate 142*). More commonly, one has to retreat well back from the line, prime examples of which are *Plates 129, 137* and *161*.

Plate 36: Railway bridges over roads are seldom suitable for steam photographs. Over water, however, they can be picturesque, provided that a suitable viewpoint can be found. North of Goudhurst, this broad-side uses the River Teise plus its reeds, meadow, trees and a steel-girder bridge on brick abutments. They frame an SECR class H tank with push–pull set, apparently passing beneath an SER loading-gauge. The windows, doors and corridor are clear-cut on the leading LSWR composite, conjuring up images of long journeys to the West Country during *La Belle Époche* of 1900–14. In his painting *Riverside Local*, Don Breckon uses a similar setting on an imaginary GWR branch, but adding a pub, cars, farm track and people to the right-hand bank (*Reference 8*, p. viii).

Plate 37 (*opposite, above*): The Plymouth, Devonport and South Western Junction Railway (PD&SWJR) main line kept to the east of the River Tamar but crossed several major tributaries. The Tavy viaduct was built with eight spans of steel truss plus stone arches at either end, made all the lovelier by the curvature. From a modestly elevated viewpoint at one end, a spectacular setting evolves, with an 'echo effect' of two patches of tidal water to the left and right. The extended bunker of LSWR class M7 tank No. 30036 leads the way to Plymouth for a three-coach set of Maunsells. The half-crewman is a bonus but there is no visible exhaust or cloud-colour.

Plate 38 (*opposite, below*): One of the tallest viaducts on the Southern is at Calstock on the Callington branch of the PD&SWJR. Built of concrete blocks to a height of 120 ft, it crosses the Tamar Valley on twelve graceful arches. From this elevated viewpoint, the whole landscape opens up, showing to full advantage the valley, town, far hillside and the viaduct itself. The tiny train, barely noticeable, is headed by an Ivatt 2–6–2 tank. The white houses, small boats, trees and patchwork of fields are a delight. The original railway here was the narrow-gauge East Cornwall Mineral which ran from the quay (far bank) up a cable-operated incline to Kelly Bray. Opened in 1872, it was taken over by the PD&SWJR in 1891. Both this and the Tavy viaduct remain in service to this day.

Plate 40: At Brixton, a long single span carries the LBSCR's South London Line over the LCDR main line and platforms. The great lattice side-trusses provide a perfect setting to portray Down expresses to the Kent coast. This boat train is headed by 'Battle of Britain' class Pacific No. 34088, *213 Squadron*, looking far too big to clear the bridge (although the fireman looks unperturbed). Framing is completed by the cross-brace (top left), platform fences, a Camp Coffee poster and enamelled Wright's Coal Tar Soap signs. You can smell the aroma!

Plate 41: Sevenoaks also has a spectacular skew bridge but with four short spans (one for each line) carrying the A21 trunk road. It is a much lighter (and cheaper) structure than Brixton's, comprising simple steel beams on stone piers. The 'engine too big' illusion is again evident and framing is completed by a stately SR signal bracket, several lamps and an SR enamelled station name-sign. The Down boat train is headed by 'West Country' class Pacific No. 34103 *Calstock* – the Southern's generous tribute to the remote country town seen in *Plate 38*.

Plate 39 (*opposite*): The River Stour in Dorset offers a perfect reflection of trees and masonry. Rivers are seldom as placid as this. Four brick arches and a central under-truss of steel carry the Somerset & Dorset main line with a north-bound train of Great Western stock. This is a portrait of a civil engineering wonder. In terms of composition, it is the river which supports the viaduct, framed also by foreground undergrowth, distant trees, cloud colour, a trail of steam and the humble train. It is a restful scene, evoking fond memories of the S&D.

Plate 44: In silhouette, the skewed road bridge at Axminster provides a graceful, parabolic frame of stone. It focuses our attention upon the immaculate engine, 'Merchant Navy' class Pacific No. 35026 *Lamport & Holt Line*, ready to depart with a train to Waterloo. Framing is completed by the raised signal, enclosed footbridge, Down canopy and platform, empty but for the lone passenger. The deep shadows and rich texture effects are created by the up-sun aspect. Dense, wafting exhaust suggests that stoking is in progress.

Plate 42 (*opposite, above*): Like a John le Carré plot, there are three levels of concentric framing at Yeovil Town: first, the front girder, its bracket and GWR foreground signals; second, the square aperture of the far end of the bridge; and third, the far signals – SR at 'stop' and GWR at 'off'. Items of added interest are the bicycle, grindstone and SR platelayers' hut. They frame LSWR class M7 tank No. 30131, working up with much smoke from Pen Mill with a push-pull set, and shortly to take the graceful curve (right) to Yeovil Junction. The scene is so tidy!

Plate 43 (*opposite, below*): The silhouetted outline of a footbridge is used for top-framing at Evercreech Junction, completed by the S&D canopied shelter (left) and the stone-built station building (right). It is a powerful portrait of big BR locomotives – class 5MT No. 73054 and class 9F No. 92210 – issuing several wisps of steam. They are made to look all the more powerful by the up-sun aspect with deep shadow effects. Railway artists Chris Woods, Terence Cuneo and others have produced similar portraits of engines in this full-frontal style.

Plate 45: Precise camera positioning was necessary for this complex composition at Poole. Peripheral items dominate, including the lattice footbridge, platform canopy, enamelled BR sign, bike, waiting pedestrians, crossing gates and box,

a paling fence, lorry, tall pole, various commercial buildings and a gas-holder. They frame standard class 4MT No. 75007 at the head of a train from Bournemouth West, bound for the S&D line to Bath.

Plate 46: A strongly horizontal composition at Eastleigh where six railway tracks are crossed by two long, single-span bridges: first, an SR lattice gantry with electric route indicators for the starting signals; beyond, a road bridge of plate girder construction – note how the top flange is thicker in the middle (like a leaf spring). They frame SR 'Lord Nelson' class 4–6–0 No. 30861 *Lord Anson*, making smoke on an express to Bournemouth. Visual stops include the bridge columns (right), a brick hut (left) and multi-spar telegraph pole. Note the visual 'ricochet' between the ground-signals, headcode discs and track-circuit diamonds. The pointwork is a delight.

Plate 47: A geometric study at Tonbridge, with strong diagonals and a massive over-bridge which carries the A21 trunk road as well as the main station building. Spanning five tracks on individual arches, it serves as a symbolic gateway to the Wealden plain. Note the windowed cross-corridor and the Down starting signals. Platform canopies, two track-walkers and an SECR coach complete the framing of a steamy class N Mogul No. 31826. The low morning side-light creates rich shadow effects, including a grotesquely distorted water-column on the tender. It is a spacious railway scene with much 'atmosphere', requiring precise positioning of the camera.

Plate 48: A study of shadows near Mayfield, featuring standard class 4MT tank No. 80015 on a train to Tunbridge Wells West. The silhouetted arc of a road bridge provides the principal framing, balanced by the cutting, grasses and wooden fence on the right. Side-light brings out detail on the front of the engine as well as a complete shadow of the train in the space left for possible doubling of the line. Although lacking steam exhaust, the central copse of trees acts as a sort of substitute. It is a warm country scene, evoking fond memories of this unhurried, double-ended, cross-country line which guarded the eastern border of the LBSCR empire.

Sweet 'Cuckoo' line, a winding cord from Redgate Mill, a patchwork Field
Of Rother, May and Heath, we steam to Polegate through the sylvan Weald;
Drift gently down via Hellingly and red-tiled Hams of Hor and Hail;
Sweet Sussex journey, 'Brighton' style, to Eastbourne's railway terminal.

(Author)

Plate 49: The LBSCR did not shrink from major investment in infrastructure on its four lines to East Grinstead. The spur from the high-level to St Margaret's junction was an after-thought, requiring a deep, steep cutting through unstable Wealden sub-soils. One result was this spectacular brick retaining wall, reinforced with buttresses and alcoves, abutted by a fine brick over-bridge. Note the recesses and ornamentation. Photographed up-sun, they provide a strong framework for LBSCR 0–6–0 class C2X No. 32521, running light on a complex reversing sequence via the high- and low-levels. Introduced by Robert Billinton in 1893, the class was rebuilt by Douglas Marsh from 1908. The large spectacle stands out like a dinner-plate above the darkened boiler.

Plate 50 (*opposite*): A study of bulk at Verwood, featuring the exchange of tokens on a train to Salisbury. Principal framing is provided by the sooty brick over-bridge and the high-rave BR tender of standard class 4 Mogul No. 76054. Supporting features are the barrow-crossing with SR warning sign, an LSWR oil lamp on its barley-sugar standard, and a lower-quadrant starting signal on an LSWR lattice post. Human activity is the central interest, although the crewman and signalman look like dwarves in this setting. There is a glimpse of the single line ahead. It is sobering to consider the massive capital investment required to bring such a line of modest traffic across rural Wessex. The investment was probably never repaid but it did keep the GWR at bay.

Plate 53: A sunny scene near Shanklin at the start of the formidable 1 in 70 Apse Bank to Wroxall. Voluminous cotton-wool exhaust rises from the tall chimney of LSWR class O2 tank No. 31 *Chale* at the head of a rake of LBSCR coaches. They are framed by the elegant brick bridge, a concrete platelayers' hut, grassy banks, trees, clouds and the sinister skyline crucifix of a telegraph pole. But the old locomotive steals the show, immaculately clean.

Plate 51 (*opposite, above*): Trains emerging from over-bridges can be spectacular if they are making steam. On the SER main line near Smeeth, 4–4–0 class D1 No. 31489 bursts forth with great billows of exhaust on a crisp spring morning. The bridge itself has form but little detail. Framing is completed by trees, fences and a mile-post (57¼). We focus upon the elegant lines of the SECR express engine, a class introduced by Harry Wainwright in 1901 but rebuilt and superheated by Richard Maunsell from 1921. They served well until electrification in 1961.

Plate 52 (*opposite, below*): An elevated viewpoint portrays this majestic brick road bridge carrying a farm track over the SER main line east of Tonbridge. Charging through with a long trail of steam is rebuilt 'West Country' class Pacific No. 34016 *Bodmin*, on a train to the Channel ports. Sandy banks and winter trees complete the picture.

Plate 54: Tunnels make fine settings for steam trains but can be overpowering or ungainly if photographed too close or without care. This cutting appears cool, lush and verdant at the north end of Sevenoaks tunnel. From a high viewpoint, rich undergrowth and trees are combined with the portal to frame SECR class H tank No. 31177, propelling an SECR push–pull set into the black hole with a wispy trail of steam. Side-sun brings texture to the foreground ferns and bunker coal, but the portal remains in shadow – mysterious. Tunnel electrification equipment litters the lineside. We remain in awe of the Victorian navvies who first toiled here in the 1860s.

Plate 56: Heathfield tunnel is the setting for standard 2–6–4 class 4MT tank No. 80149, heading a train of LBSCR stock to Tunbridge Wells West. Something has caught the attention of the driver and passengers who are leaning out, bringing the picture to life. While this colourful train dominates the foreground, it is the portal which truly fires our imagination, its bright variegated brickwork contrasting with the black, elliptical hole.

Plate 55 (*opposite, below*): When the Bath end of the S&D was doubled, additional single-track tunnels were bored through the Mendip hills. The twin portals and approach cuttings at Windsor Hill make an intriguing setting for LMS 0–6–0 class 4F No. 44559 with a south-bound local train. Additional features are the catch-point, several signs, concrete fences and a platelayers' hut. Trees and the overland telegraph complete the scene. The cost of this extension crippled the S&D financially, resulting in the takeover by the LSWR and the Midland Railway.

Plate 57: Argos Hill tunnel (near Rotherfield) is short and shallow, no doubt built by the cut-and-cover method. Enriched by mixed woodland, this grassy approach cutting provides a fine setting for standard 2–6–4 tank No. 80153, making a little smoke on a train to Eastbourne. Using an elevated viewpoint with side-sun, the result is a warm, balanced composition. Interest focuses upon the engine, SR van and LBSCR coaches – their roof profiles becoming progressively lower. For comparison, one of Hamilton Ellis' paintings in *Reference 1*, p. viii depicts an LBSCR train on this line from around 1885, featuring Craven 2–2–2 locomotive *Southsea* and a Stroudley six-wheel saloon.

Plate 58 (*opposite, above*): Penge tunnel is a mile and a quarter long, bored through London clay. The massive west portal provides a sinister frame for SECR 4–4–0 class D1 No. 31749, running light into Sydenham Hill station. Low morning side-sun picks out engine side and driver, also the SR 'art deco' electric lamp, concrete standard, silhouetted trees and a jumble of signalry and posts on the left, shortly before the conversion to colour-lights. Shapes on the engine are intriguing, especially the spectacles, square firebox, splasher and bi-level running plate.

Plate 59 (*opposite, below*): Oxted tunnel is a mile long, bored through chalk. Its smoky south portal is a small but important part of this North Downs landscape. The great hill and shallow-angled cutting frame an Up train at speed, headed by standard 2–6–4 tank No. 80143. Timing was important to capture just enough of the train without losing the scenery. We can explore the immaculate black loco, the guard's ducket and other detail on the Maunsell flat-sided coach. Weak winter sun adds texture to the foreground grasses and to the trees on the left.

4. People and Locomotion

There are more people in this book than locomotives, being clearly visible in 44 per cent of the pictures. They range from the peering half-face of a driver, to platforms splattered with waiting passengers or teeming with railwaymen as trains are emptied, serviced and 'run-round'. Occasionally, people will pose for a photograph, but more often, they must be captured at opportunist moments, as a press photographer would work.

On busy stations, people can get in the way of train pictures. In such situations, the sensible solution is to abandon train photography and concentrate instead upon the people. More often than not, they enhance the scene, reminding us that railways are run *by* people and *for* people. By careful selection of viewpoint, often hurriedly in order to 'catch the moment', people will bring a picture to life, either as 'framing auxiliaries' or as the focus of attention. Examples of the latter are enthusiasts gazing into a cab, a firemen 'bunker-trimming', or the exchange of the single-line token. This chapter shows the token exchange using staffs and hoops, both common on the Southern.

In the confined space of a signal-box, the signalman is usually the focus of attention, although *Plate 81* shows that this is not always the case. Signalmen outside their boxes always enhance the scene, whether on the cat-walk or by the track. Between boxes, trackmen are king. Of their various grades, Linesmen carry out minor track maintenance (to the instructions of Lengthsmen) and cut the lineside grass and undergrowth, 'firing' it every few years. Linesmen also assist with major track renewals at weekends and at night, working under Platelayers. Lengthsmen walk the track (daily on busy lines), carrying a track gauge and marking sleepers for re-alignments, renewals or whatever. Pictorially, trackmen are often treated as auxiliaries but being such interesting characters, group-portraits can be admirable, adorned with the tools of their trade. All had a wealth of railway tales to tell, most of it now lost.

On moving trains, crewmen and passengers are unpredictable. Some lean or wave deliberately when they spot the camera, joining in the spirit of the occasion. The passengers always have smiling faces, enjoying the sensation of line-riding with the wind on their faces and the clackety-clack of rail-joints beneath the wheels. In yards, shunters can be captured at work although such pictures are rare. Railway clerks, managers, planners and other office workers are seldom photographed since they are remote from the scenes of action. This is a pity because they all have a role to play and interesting tales to tell. The author regrets never photographing a booking clerk in his 'glory hole', with a multiplicity of ticket racks and cubby-holes of railway literature.

Railway enthusiasts come in a variety of guises. Many start engine-spotting as young lads, using Ian Allan's excellent series *British Railway Locomotives* for reference, and later evolving into locomotive experts – rivet by rivet in many cases. Those who evolve from model railways tend to take a catholic interest in the railway scene as a whole, often becoming fine photographers. Then there are the historians, capable of reeling off stories and statistics of lines and train services throughout the world – invaluable people in small doses! The railway clubs and societies foster armies of correspondents and travellers who ride the 'steam specials' and visit the preserved lines – havens of the most revered of enthusiasts. Preservationists rightly receive the highest accolades because they 'do' rather than just observe the steam railway.

Plate 60: Railway enthusiasts come in all shapes, sizes and ages. At Edenbridge Town, two lads in duffel coats study the footplate of an 0–4–4 class H tank, photographed by a smart-looking gent in a raincoat and flat cap. The triangular canopy and neat awning contrast with the coal lumps and the pagoda curvature of the Wainwright cab.

Plate 62: Many railway enthusiasts begin as a humble engine spotters, tending to congregate on major junction stations. Something has caught the attention of this group, waiting eagerly at Eastleigh, pencils and notebooks in hand. For the moment, they are ignoring the lovely old 4–6–0 locomotive with its high arched cab, steaming gently through the yard with the exhaust looking dark against light cloud cover. Class H15 No. 30475 was a Maunsell variation of an LSWR design. The seat is LSWR, the barrow and lamps are SR, and the enamelled sign is BR.

Plate 61 (*opposite*): At Sheffield Park, families enjoy a day out on the Bluebell Railway during the pioneering years of steam preservation. They witness the departure of Adams 4–4–2 'radial' tank No. 488 in LSWR livery, on a train to Horsted Keynes. The leading coach is an LNWR observation saloon. The concrete track is BR but the tapered wooden signals and posts are LBSCR – well maintained over some four decades by the SR and BR. Passenger access between platforms at that time was via the barrow crossing, controlled by station staff.

Plate 63: Between trains at Rowfant, a spell of juvenile conversation and leg-dangling, adding to the run-stripes of white paint at the platform edge. No one hurried much on this single-track, double-ended, half-forgotten branch line across north Sussex. The woods are a delight, so too the building whose unique, cottage-style architecture was to satisfy the local landowner who gave the land. Note the porch, eaves and bargeboards, chimneys, ornate windows, oil lamps, SR enamelled signs, bells, ladder and paling fence. The rear board and supports for the SR name-sign are LBSCR. The whitening around the entrance portal is no doubt a relic from the war-time blackout. BR made little impact here until dieselization in 1963 and line closure in 1967.

Plate 65 (*opposite, below*): At Halwill, smiling passengers have arrived on a train from Padstow. The locomotive too has a pleasant smile which the Revd Audrey might have exploited for his illustrated children's books. Drummond 4–4–0 class T9 had the nickname 'Greyhound', built for speed on LSWR expresses. No. 30715 has the later modification of a stove-pipe chimney. Looking fairly smart in BR black, its clean lines are admirable, broken by the graceful curve of the splasher and the flared rave of the eight-wheel tender. A Mogul stands on the Down line, alongside the Maunsell coaches. Were the happy travellers visiting relatives in this remote spot, one wonders?

Plate 64: A study of connections at Wareham. Passengers from the Swanage branch train are preparing to board the Bournemouth train, now arriving in platform 3. There is time for a chat or to tidy one's hair. Although the two boiler diameters are the same, standard class 4 Mogul No. 76008 has its boiler set much higher than Drummond 0–4–4 class M7 tank No. 30108. Their age difference was about fifty-five years but the class numbers built were similar, respectively 115 and 105. The LSWR canopy is both smart and functional, giving comprehensive cover. Note the telegraph connections for bells and phones. The branch train will shortly transfer to platform 1.

Plate 66: The cab of a 'Terrier' tank catches the attention of a young couple at Hayling Island. LBSCR No. 61 *Sutton* retains its Stroudley tool box proudly at the rear. Note the extended bunker, coal on the roof and the immaculate Maunsell coaches.

Plate 67 (*below*): At Hawkhurst, the cab of a Wainwright tank engine captures the imagination of a young enthusiast. His mother, however, appears unimpressed as a fireman performs acrobatic feats along the roof. Built for SECR commuter service, some class H tanks were granted an extended life in push–pull mode. Although No. 31266 is dirty, its quaint profile stands out, so too the externally mounted pumps for vacuum brakes and the air-controlled push–pull system. Note the barrows, oil lamps and wooden underside of the integral canopy.

Plate 68: A young booted admirer of a Stroudley masterpiece at Hayling Island. He is captivated by the open firebox door, the swathes of extraneous steam and the cab-mounted brake-pump whose shaft is slowly reciprocating. 'Terrier' tank No. 32677 has reversed on to the train of BR non-corridor stock. Built in 1880, this 0–6–0 was LBSCR No. 77 *Wonersh*. It was re-named *Carisbrooke* from 1927 until 1949 during service on the Isle of Wight, and was scrapped in 1959. Compared with *Sutton* in *Plate 66*, the bunker has been extended rearwards but only two panels taller. The composition is a dialogue between boy and machine, framed by the coach and awning, to create a triangle of visual interest and contrasts. The role of the bucket is uncertain.

Plate 71: On the LSWR's prestige route to Plymouth, the arrival at Bere Alston of an Up train, framed by two platforms which are teeming with people. On the left, passengers are rushing in all directions, alighting or about to board, including a National Serviceman in battle-dress, hand-in-hand with his sweetheart – did they ever marry? This busy scene contrasts with that on the far platform where passengers wait patiently, the girls in full-skirted dresses which were so fashionable during the late 1950s. They are framed and protected by the great wooden canopy and the stone PD&SWJR station building whose slated roof is hipped at one end and gabled at the other. Note the neat chimney-pots, the stone 'gents' and the red telephone box. The train of Maunsell stock is clean and smart, headed by an unidentified Mogul. This 'stationscape' is facilitated by the elevated viewpoint, halfway up the footbridge. Such varied subject matter would not have been be visible from platform level.

Plate 69 (*opposite, above*): Passengers descend from Gunnislake's island platform, pushing a pram and a bicycle. Another pauses to admire an Ivatt 2–6–2 class 2 tank which heads a train to Bere Alston. This Dartmoor scene has a cosmopolitan feel, with SR name-signs, an LMS engine, SECR coaches and a seven-plank open wagon from the Eastern Region. The coaches are ten-compartment seconds, each coupled to a Maunsell corridor brake-composite to form a 'W' set. In terms of composition, a short stretch of platform has become centre-stage for people, framed by a wealth of railway interest. What a wonder that the railway served such a bleak plateau!

Plate 70 (*opposite, below*): The story of an arrival at Deepdene. Wearing uniforms from the late steam age, Girl Guides and a Boy Scout surrender tickets to a railwayman in shirt-sleeves and braces. They are probably *en route* to Box Hill, seen top-left in the picture. This elevated station has an SER wooden building with hipped roof and brick chimney. The unusual canopy is flat and propped from the front of the building and with minimal valancing. Note the clean-looking BR enamelled signs, the sand-bin and a row of colourful posters along the fence. Framing is completed by the Maunsell rear-end, as the train re-starts towards Redhill with a nice plume of steam.

Plate 72: Saturday morning at Sheerness-on-Sea, with a carriage-load of ladies returning from a shopping trip to Sittingbourne, complete with straw bags, children and pushchairs. They are framed by the massive LCDR cantilevered canopy, together with its support columns, brackets, SR gas lamps and SECR 0–6–0 class C No. 31495, making gentle steam on the left. This lovely Wainwright goods engine provides a visual stop and reference point to counter the movement of the passengers. But the ladies steal the show – they look so happy! Sadly, the end is nigh for the three steam trains in this picture, for the third rail is laid, ready for E-day.

Plate 74 (*opposite, below*): A lone passenger stands in the vast emptiness of Dover Priory. His attention is drawn to the coupling of SR 0–6–0 class Q1 No. 33037 to the rear of a train of BR Mark 1 stock – resplendent in crimson, cream and sunshine. Massive framing is provided by the dark canopy, its supports, SR covered steel footbridge, the White Cliffs and the Bulleid tri-level tender with its characteristic hook-over rear ladder, semi-shrouded in extraneous steam. Note also the fireman's hose, front engine and long tunnel through to the docks. But it is the man in the suit who grips our attention. Like *Felix the Cat* cartoons, one can almost see a dotted line from his eyes to a greasy railwayman working at track level. His protuberant cigarette was common in the age of steam.

Plate 73: Conversation with a sailor in the Hastings bay at Ashford, framed by the SECR canopy and a local train. The rear coach is LSWR with an SR push-pull cab. In some strange transpositions of rolling stock, we can also find SECR coaches in the far south-west (*Plate 69*).

Plate 75: In this action-packed composition at Havant, centre-stage is shared by busy people and an LBSCR 'Terrier' tank. 'Hayling Billy' has shortly arrived with a train of BR non-corridor stock. Passengers are boarding, uncoupling is in progress and there is a conversation on the footplate of No. 32677, barely audible above the noise of the blowing safety valve. Cab geometry and spectacles are clear Stroudley characteristics, but his toolbox has been lost due to the bunker extension. Note the bucket on the lamp-iron and the lamps on the side-tank. The buffer-stop, terraced houses, warehouse and coach provide framing. It was sad for everyone in the picture when the branch closed in 1963. To ride the Hayling line was to enjoy a time-capsule of Stroudleyana.

Plate 77: At Torrington, railwaymen outnumber passengers following the arrival of a train from Barnstaple. LMS 2–6–2 class 2 tank No. 41297 is almost obscured by steam as the cylinder drain cocks are opened – the roar is deafening! The station was re-modelled in 1925, so most of the platform accessories are SR, as are the coaches. This bold composition focuses upon the two railwaymen by the central stop-signal (which is post-1945). Framing is provided by the steam, the station building and a row of 'art-deco' electric lamps on concrete standards. None of these dominates, however, since the viewpoint is elevated, opening up the scene to reveal everything. The central character in dirty overalls, belt, jacket and cap, looks a true disciple of the Age of Steam.

Plate 76 (*opposite, below*): Between 1923 and 1949, twenty-three LSWR 0–4–4 class O2 tanks were transferred to the Isle of Wight. They had their bunkers enlarged for intensive Island service, giving a 'flat-iron' impression. Another modification for seasonal holiday traffic was the extended guard/luggage compartment, seen here to occupy half the leading SECR brake-third. Beneath a great cloud of safety valve steam, No. 17 *Seaview* departs Havenstreet for Ryde. The leaning crewman directs our gaze to the gaggle of alighted passengers who are shortly to be escorted across the track. They are in suspended animation, passing the time in conversation and captured by the elevated camera. None is a holidaymaker. The telegraph provides framing but is a distraction in this instance.

Plate 78: Track maintenance workers are known as linesmen. As well as repairing the track, they cut lineside trees, undergrowth and grass, 'firing' it every few years. This straightforward group-portrait uses natural stances and expressions, but includes a sickle, grindstone, grass and track to establish their occupation. Working between Wareham and Wool they are (left to right) Stan Smith, Arthur 'Art' Welsh and Leo 'Len' Burden. Len is the ganger (or chargehand), wearing a three-piece suit and trilby. He was a third generation railwayman on this section.

Plate 79 (*opposite, above*): Platform canopies and two railwaymen frame a train at Newport, headed by LSWR class O2 tank No. 31 *Chale*, displaying its rear number-plate. Bright sunlight brings out some nice tones on the locomotive but people once again steal the show. Unanswered questions include: Why is the stationman (left) adjusting his hat? What is the guard (right) waiting for? Why doesn't someone move the pile of mail sacks? Where are the train crew? What is happening in the 'Freshwater bay' (distant left)? See *Plate 90* for one answer.

Plate 80 (*opposite, below*): A cock-eyed telegraph pole and some wicked-looking scythes and sickles are used in this portrait of friendly linesmen near Daggons Road. Left to right, they are A. Edsall, Jack Mussell and Frank King. All are in shirt-sleeve order, two have bib-and braces overalls with front pockets, all have belts (one of string) and two have trousers tied at the ankles. As in *Plate 78*, their hats are an interesting mix of trilby, beret and flat cap (cheese-cutter). Their work was idyllic on warm, dry days. There was great camaraderie.

Plate 82: Action at Sheffield Park, with the 'Wealden Rambler' emerging from sidings into the Up platform. The scene is colourful not only for the restored locomotives, but also for the framework of foreground signs, chain, water-tower and LBSCR shunting signals. Note also the 'echo effect' of the stored locos and coach on the far tracks. Motion and life are provided by the smoke, low-level steam and crewmen – both leaning out to watch the crowded platform ahead. Twenty-five years separate the locomotives: Wainwright 0–6–0 class P tank (SECR No. 27 in dark green, fully lined and with a polished brass dome) was built in 1910; while Adams 4–4–2 'radial' tank (LSWR No. 488 in a lighter shade of green with less elaborate lining) was built in 1885. They are a credit to the early preservationists. A wealth of locomotives and rolling stock can be found in various states of restoration and readiness in the yards and sidings of the Bluebell line. The volunteer drivers are clearly enjoying themselves.

> Pause awhile, take in the scene, but do not pass this point,
> The magic of the Bluebell line will never disappoint;
> But do take heed, no 'right to roam', our signs and chains inhibit,
> And should you cross, you will become a permanent exhibit.
>
> (*Author*)

Plate 81 (*opposite*): Careful camera positioning and fine adjustment of Depth of Field were needed to portray this signalman at Ashurst junction. The lever arms and frame have immaculate metallic sheens, dominating the composition. His shoes also shine but the railwayman is relegated here to a secondary role, helping to 'frame the frame', along with his bucket, token release instrument, clock, oil and electric lamps and telegraph instruments along the block shelf. The electric token instrument is of the Webb & Thompson type, holding a stack of staffs for the single line to East Grinstead. Footboard wear is from generations of working lives spent in this haven of peace.

Plate 84: Shanklin's signalman in blue serge stands ready for the split-second exchange of single-line tablets, enclosed in leather pouches having steel hoops. LSWR class O2 tank No. 25 *Godshill* arrives with a train of LBSCR stock bound for Ventnor while No. 31 *Chale* awaits its turn on the single track to Sandown. A whiff of chimney smoke stands out against the rich tones of cloud cover, while strong in-line sunlight brings out the panelling and fittings of SECR brake-third No. S4149. Framing is completed by the right-hand group of trolleys, poles and extraneous railwaymen. All is clean and tidy. The dome and tank-side of No. 25 are gleaming.

Plate 83 (*opposite, above*): A wooden platform was provided at Redgate Mill junction for the exchange of the single-line staff for the 'Cuckoo' line. The signalman is framed by his Saxby & Farmer box and by the train – standard class 4 tank No. 80015 – heading an incongruous mix of BR Mark 1 and LBSCR (push–pull) stock. The train tapers almost to nothing at the platelayers' hut on the left. The crewman's wave is a bonus, helping to offset the bland bulk of the tall bunker. Note the bunker coal, piled high, the diagonal row of buckets and what looks like a floodlight above the stairway. After perusal, our attention always returns to the raised arm of the alert signalman.

Plate 85 (*above*): The SECR signal-box at Ryde St John's Road was transferred from Waterloo Junction in 1928. Spacious and well-lit by tall windows, daylight reflects from the linoleum, painted woodwork and various fittings of brass and steel. Mr Dick Russel was one of two railway brothers. He is portrayed in the act of pulling, framed by most of his equipment – tool-box (bottom left), hanging coats, suspended lamps (oil and electric), fire buckets, telegraph instruments, loudhailer, long tools, stove and the levers. Compared with *Plate 81*, the signal-frame is less dominant since the camera is further away at the side. We focus upon his hands and cloth, anticipating the crash of the lever and the ring of a bell above the gentle simmering of the kettle. Then all is peace again.

Plate 86 (*next page*): A highly 'atmospheric' study at Cranleigh, with a column of safety-valve steam and early morning mist lingering in the conifers. LSWR class M7 tank No. 30049 arrives with a train to Guildford, while SECR class H tank No. 31543 awaits its turn on the single track to Horsham. We focus upon the surrender of the token, a juggling act which is compelling to watch – will the staff drop the staff? Five people and a bicycle bring the scene to life. Comprehensive framing includes the silhouetted valance and lamp, the squat signal-box, tall trees and the SECR coach (left). Note the graceful curve of the platform, its whitened edge leading the eye to the elderly signalman. This composition required accurate camera positioning, fine focusing and perfect timing.

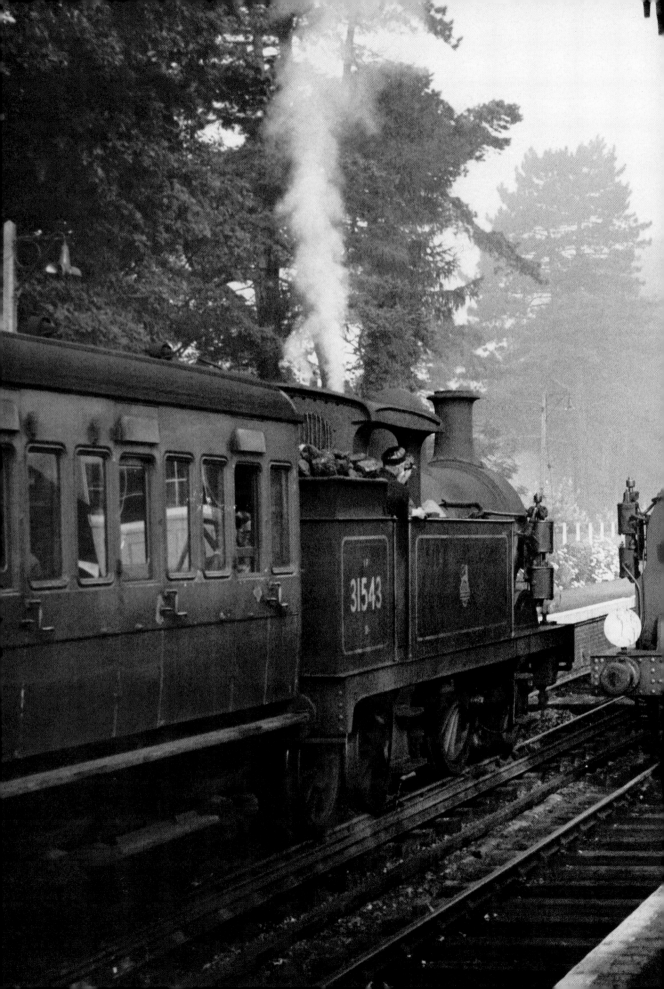

Plate 87: The unrebuilt 'Merchant Navy' class was arguably the best-looking of the Bulleid Pacifics, although No. 35028 *Clan Line* has un-level numbering. Looking immaculately clean, its high-rave tender blends well with the cab, boiler cladding and smoke deflector. Drawing into Eastleigh's Up platform, it is framed by the multiple tracks, white Italianate station building, multi-spar telegraph and the LNER parcels van. Light smoke and safety-valve steam provide a sense of motion. The crewman and a packed platform bring the scene to life.

Plate 88: An attempt at Herne Hill to frame a Down boat train between two sets of signals. To avoid obscuring the driver, however, the shutter release was delayed by a fraction of a second. The outcome is a somewhat dominant engine-front from which colour-lights are sprouting! The colourful train nevertheless retains its charm, headed by 'Battle of Britain' class Pacific No. 34089 *602 Squadron* (which flew Spitfires based in Glasgow).

Plate 89: The Battle of Britain is again commemorated, this time at Victoria with No. 34087 *145 Squadron* (which flew Hurricanes from Westhampnett, Sussex). A fireman affixes headcode discs and train numbering while the driver is in deep conversation with station staff. The steam relief column is offset to avoid unstable 'duality', revealing the untidy detail of the SECR station (right). The LBSCR station (left) looks immaculate.

Plate 90: Water-filling at Newport, with a fireman operating the valve chain from the running plate. Class O2 tank No. 35 *Freshwater* is on shunting duty, standing (appropriately) in the former 'Freshwater bay' whose starting signal and doll were removed from the signal bracket following branch closure in 1953. This was an unusual, unstable-looking water-tank design for the Southern – a 'baked bean can' perched upon a single support pedestal. The water arm could also swing to the right to serve the Cowes platform. Note the brazier below complete with long flue.

Plate 91: There is no water tank on the platform at Maidstone East, but there is a crude brazier. The buried water valve has a hand-wheel extension alongside the LCDR column with its characteristic swan-neck filler. The crew of standard 2–6–4 tank No. 80087 are busy with watering and bunker-trimming, preparing for the final haul on this Ashford to Victoria service. The concrete lamp standard is an unfortunate visual intrusion, but there is an enticing view past the SR signal to the Medway bridge beyond. The post is unusually tall for a rail-built design.

Plate 92: Railway artists can add drivers and other people 'at will'. Railway photographers, on the other hand, have to be patient and ready to snap up 'people opportunities'. Such was the case at Victoria, with the 'Golden Arrow' ready to depart from platform 8, headed by 'Battle of Britain' class Pacific No. 34085 *501 Squadron*. The great arrow shows up vividly on the smooth side of the Bulleid casing, emphasized in the reflected light. Framing is provided by the van and warehouse (left) and by a long backcloth of tall houses (see also *Plate 109*).

Plate 93: Photographs of manual shunting operations are rare. With the phasing-out of the three-link coupling and individually assigned wagons, they are now historic. At Southampton Docks, an old-fashioned shunter is caught in the act of poling the coupling of a BR covered wagon. He is the focus of attention, framed by a loading gauge and observed by the young driver of LSWR class C14 tank No. 77s. One can imagine them playing all morning. This Hornbyesque steam loco was one of the smallest in BR service, the sole survivor of a batch of 2–2–0 tanks introduced by Dugald Drummond in 1906. Each was integral with a coach body to make a motor-train, used principally on the East Southsea branch. They were converted by Robert Urie in 1923 into 0–4–0 service locos.

Plate 95: A clear technical record at Eastleigh of a fine standard BR locomotive, 4–6–0 class 5MT No. 73119, featuring its enclosed cab, 'wheel motion' and high running plate. Note the speedometer generator and cabling on the rear wheel, also the coal on the step and neat rows of riveting on the cab and high-rave tender. In this perspective, the square firebox looks disproportionately large for the boiler. An imminent departure southwards is suggested by the swirling steam at the front and the raised signal arm above – the unfocused gantry being an important part of the framing. It is the driver who brings the scene to life – his congenial face, clasped hands and shiny peaked cap inspiring confidence in any observer. We know that we are in safe hands, so let us ride on!

Plate 94 (*opposite, below*): West of High Halstow Halt and lacking a headcode, class H tank No. 31193 'emerges from grasses' with a train of Maunsells. Framing is completed by a neat row of poplars, other trees, fence posts and a telegraph pole. Coals are piled high in the bunker. Exhaust smoke and steam provide a sense of motion. It is the driver, however, who brings life to the scene with his shining cap, smiling face and bare arms. There is also a glimpse of passengers at the open windows in the middle coach. A technical record of a train service is therefore transformed into a story of people having a 'day out'. Their destination is Allhallows-on-Sea, a somewhat overstated name for a Thameside estuarine resort which the SR promoted with its new sub-branch.

5. Station Panoramas

Stations offer fine settings for steam because they are packed with interesting buildings, canopies, people, associated yards, signalry and a wealth of furniture and appendages. Any or all of these can be incorporated into creative compositions, with the train either dominant or ancillary. This chapter shows examples of both, but concentrates especially upon the 'station panorama' which covers most of the station, often with an element of external environment – scenery, town buildings, vehicles or whatever. Such compositions can be studied at length, offering the complete experience of arriving at a station, waiting on the platform and catching the train.

Most of the stations shown are rural, and most are now closed. The demise of the rural station is sad. They were wonderful places to sit and ponder, combining Victorian splendour with the peace and greenness of the countryside. City stations are much greyer and noisier, represented here by just Salisbury and Victoria. The latter is a reminder of a conundrum – what is the next logical station in the sequence: London Bridge, Bricklayers Arms, Charing Cross, Victoria, Waterloo . . . ? For a clue, see *Plate 92*.

Subsidiary items in 'station panoramas' include barrows, seats, people, signs, advertisements, lamps, fire-buckets, TV aerials (VHF), telegraph poles, signal-boxes, fences, huts, footbridges, loading gauges, stretcher-cupboards, water-columns and signals. While none may be dominant, each contributes to compositional balance and broadens the railway interest. A full historical record needs such items.

The Age of Steam was also the Age of Coal. For a century and a half, 'King Coal' reigned supreme, not only for locomotion but for stationary engines, power stations, gas works, iron-and-steel works, stoves and open-grate fires. Whereas domestic grates generally burnt bituminous coal (which is easy to light), railway stations would usually burn coke, a by-product of gas-works coal. Brick chimneys are featured in most of the pictures in this chapter, having many different styles. Earthenware pots too are often beautiful, present here in vast numbers, reminding us also of the intense pollution caused by low-level emissions. Reading like rugby football results, the chimney pot scores are: Lyme Regis 0–Partridge Green 9; Wool Wanderers 5–Evercreech Junction 9; Shepton Mallet 2–Eastleigh United 8; Brasted Halt 2–Sandown 2; Cowes 15–Victoria 77; Oakley 9–Salisbury Island Platform 8 (a close result in this local derby).

The shock result is not the 77 scored by Victoria but the 0 at Lyme Regis – with no brick chimney, how was the station heated? *Plate 96* shows three short, small-diameter pipes which are probably flues from solid-fuel stoves serving the booking office, waiting room and ladies' room. Although the station opened in 1903, post-dating the local gasworks by several decades, it was unusual to find gas heating in Edwardian stations. Following closure in 1965, the wooden shell of this building was transferred to Alresford on the Mid-Hants Railway where it now serves as a shop and buffet (electrically heated). That preserved line is best known for its range of LSWR/SR/BR locomotives and rolling stock, but its humble building from Lyme Regis may have been one of the first Southern stations without a brick chimney and pots.

The answer to the conundrum in the second paragraph is St Pancras – planned as the next London terminal for Continental passenger services via the Kent coast. The flight of the *Golden Arrow* is long spent, with *Eurostar* now in the ascendant.

Plate 96: At Lyme Regis, two photographers by the run-round loop are concentrating upon the vintage locomotive – Adams 4–4–2 'radial' tank class '0415' No. 30583. No doubt their results were excellent. By standing back and gaining elevation on the buffer-stop, however, a quite different type of picture emerges – a 'station panorama'. The wooden 'vernacular' station building is enhanced by an A30 car, telephone box, LSWR trolleys and stationmen. Trees, poles and steel mineral wagons complete the framing of this restful branch terminus.

Plate 97: This panorama at Partridge Green features an intriguing row of signal-box, station building, station-master's house and goods shed, having quite disparate architectural styles. The mid-distant push–pull train to Brighton is propelled by Drummond 0–4–4 class M7 tank No. 30049, making some nice steam but supporting rather than dominating the scene. Framed by the footbridge and canopy, railway detail includes LBSCR oil lamps, BR enamelled signs, a staff-crossing and passengers waving goodbye. The signal-box steps are enticing.

Plate 100: A powerful study of the 'Pines Express' which has just arrived at Evercreech Junction, double-headed by a standard 4–6–0 class 5MT and 2–10–0 class 9F. They are framed by the wooden canopy, steel plate footbridge, tall LSWR starting signal, stone station building with clustered chimney-pots, and an immaculate BR brake-composite in maroon. A central theme of watering and servicing is offered by the inspecting crewman and the water column. Note the huge water tank and a pile of ash beneath the brazier. The pilot will now run round to collect a following train to Templecombe. Meanwhile, our eyes follow the double-track towards Bournemouth.

Plate 98 (*opposite, above*): The gabled two-storey, white-painted, dormer-windowed station building at Wool has rustic charm, enhanced by its sloping canopy which is echoed by the wooden shelter opposite. Framed also by the telegraph and SR lamp standards, light Pacific No. 34103 *Calstock* races through with a train to Weymouth. Note the H-type TV aerial, fire buckets, unusual high-backed seats and an LSWR name-board with wooden cut-out letters. It was a pleasure waiting for the train on such a station. Were fire buckets ever used, one wonders?

Plate 99 (*opposite, below*): Using a low-camera perspective, rising vertical lines tend to converge. This can generally be corrected in the darkroom by tilting the masking frame at the front. If some of the uprights are originally divergent, however, this can produce instead a geometric conundrum. Such is the case at Wool, giving the impression of heavy banking of the track. The result is a powerful shot of a short Up train of BR Mark 1 stock headed by heavy Pacific No. 35008 *Orient Line*, nicely framed by the telegraph, signal, modern footbridge, wagons and pointwork. Compared with *Plate 98*, this panorama uses the station building in a minor role.

Plate 101: Still on the Somerset & Dorset line, a pair of standard class 4s charge through Shepton Mallet towards Bath, led by No. 75009 – the focus of our attention. A strong, deeply shadowed framework is provided by the ornate wooden canopies, a trolley collection and tracks. Operational bonuses are the two observing people, a wisp of steam below the injector and a great fug of double-exhaust which drifts down over the distant line, about to obscure the water column. We are left in no doubt that this train is approaching noisily and at speed.

Plate 102: A tranquil panorama at Ventnor, with class O2 tank No. 32 *Bonchurch* playing with carriages in the yard. A railwayman rides at the rear of an SECR third which has just uncoupled from the LBSCR coach beyond. Their contrasting roof profiles are low-elliptical and low-arc. Note the reflected evening sunlight and the framework of platform canopy, tall SR lamp standard and a great backdrop of cliff. Much of the latter is artificial, since the station was built in an old quarry, including storage caves behind the openings (right).

Plate 103: Eastleigh's spacious layout makes a fine setting for a long train of oil-tank wagons bound for the Esso refinery at Fawley. The crew of standard 2–6–2 class 3 tank No. 82015 oblige by leaning from the cab and by making steam through the exhaust and below the injector. The train is framed by the platforms, SR lamp standards, the great covered footbridge and a fine Italianate station building. Prospective passengers wait patiently. It is the long trail of white exhaust steam which brings final balance and a sense of motion.

Plate 104: A full station panorama at Brasted, enhanced by the surrounding countryside. Taken from an elevated position behind the goods yard, a grand Kentish landscape emerges, the trees and fields making the station look so small and isolated. A Maunsell push–pull train is re-starting towards Dunton Green, propelled by a class H tank with just a puff of exhaust. Mid-distant framing comprises an SER loading gauge, the left-hand hedgerow and a solitary mineral wagon. The focus of attention is not the train but the cluster of buildings, huts, coal heaps and a bonneted lorry. This oasis of civilization was a photogenic gem for enthusiasts of the full railway scene.

Plate 105: The Guildford-Horsham line was renowned for its rich countryside, well-maintained stations and vintage trains. Class H tank No. 31543 puffs into Cranleigh with a push–pull set from Horsham. Weak sunlight penetrates the morning mist and picks out the train-side, BR name-sign and white-painted platform edges. The latter, together with a low privet hedge and weed-free platforms, look immaculate, no doubt in contention for a 'best kept station' award. A tall backcloth of trees is balanced by the left-hand hedge, lamp, telegraph and starting signals – a perfect framework for the Edwardian locomotive and its crewman. The scene is harmonious.

Plate 106: At attempt at Corfe Castle to portray a fine LSWR country station in a grand landscape, taken from an adjacent hill. Unfortunately, the morning was overcast, so there is no 'enlivening texture' in the grasses, trees and undergrowth. Grandeur is nevertheless apparent in the hills and in the station building – stone-built, two-storied and gabled. A class M7 tank re-starts with a short train of Maunsells for Wareham. Closed in 1972, this line and station have been restored by Swanage Railway, running trains in Southern green and hauled by locomotives ranging from an M7 tank to a Bulleid light Pacific. Both Swanage and Corfe are fine towns to visit.

Plate 107: Sandown was a busy commuter station to Ryde as well as a prime destination for holidaymakers. At Easter 1960, however, it offered a peaceful panorama without passengers. Morning sunlight was perfect to pick out the paling fence, locomotive and concrete SR name-sign. In semi-silhouette are the SR hexagonal lamps, great platform canopies, elevated signal-box and station building. The train is a central but non-intrusive 'impression', headed appropriately by class O2 tank No. 28 *Ashey*, with Ashey Down as a backdrop (far left).

Plate 108: Cowes looks ideal for modelling, being compact, slightly curved and crammed full of interest, with yards and houses to either side of the platforms. A train of mixed SECR/LBSCR/SR stock stands ready to depart, headed by LSWR class O2 tank No. 16 *Ventnor*. It is framed by the coal merchant (left), roof-tops, intricate lattice footbridge, tall lamp and bay platform (right). Additional interest is provided by the open truck, blowing safety-valve and the run-round cross-over points. The great bunker is not over-powering and our eyes settle upon the coaches, so nicely set on the curve. Imagine them racing up to London Bridge behind a 4–4–0!

Plate 111: A bold station panorama at Oakley, using a dark, SR cast-iron Warning sign in the centre-foreground. Having no footbridge, passengers would use the wooden track-crossing from the far platform with its fine array of LSWR signal-box, lamp room, station building and canopy – note the brick extensions to the box and building. They would then follow the paling fence onto the Down platform with its thick-set telegraph poles. Passing through with a mixed freight is SR class U Mogul No. 31628, an essential but undominant part of the scene. Packed with railway interest, this is a well-balanced but busy composition, a little overpowering.

Plate 109 (*opposite, above*): The rear of a great terrace of tall houses, bristling with chimney-pots, provides a fine urban backcloth on the 'Chatham' side of Victoria. Framing is completed by the SECR signal-box and a tubular post of SR colour-light signals with an electric route indicator, a motorized shunting-disc and a spare lamp below. Centre-stage and blowing off is LSWR/ SR 4–6–0 'King Arthur' class N15 No. 30777 *Sir Lamiel*, complete with crew and a full bunker of coal. This is a true 'station panorama', not a 'man and machine' portrait (see *Plate 92*).

Plate 110 (*opposite, below*): In contrast to Victoria is the remote, uncluttered outpost of Shapwick, reached by changing at Templecombe and Evercreech Junction. The backcloth here is the cirrus sky whose wispy tones are brought out by a yellow camera filter. Framing is completed by the modern concrete platforms and an 'echo effect' using two designs of oil lamp (one S&D, the other Somerset Central, perhaps?). The train is headed by GWR Collet 0–6–0 No. 3210. The line was formerly 50 per cent owned by the SR, represented here by just the Maunsell van.

Plate 112: Class E4 'large radial passenger tank' was designed by Robert Billinton. No. 32504 entered service in 1900 as LBSCR No. 504 *Chilworth*, an interesting choice of name since that Surrey village was served by an SER station. After war service in France during 1917–19, it returned for an idyllic life, mostly on rural services until scrapping in the mid-1960s. It is pictured here at the 'wrong end' of a Maunsell push–pull set, framed by the long canopy, station building and buffer stops of Eastbourne. This graceful 0–6–2 is remarkably clean, its appearance enhanced by the enshrouding steam. Note the riveting, long coaling irons on the side-tanks and the SER-type Ramsbottom safety valves encased over the firebox.

Plate 113: 'Laurel and Hardy' pictures are great fun. Playing the roles at Salisbury are Drummond 0–4–4 class M7 tank No. 30033 and Maunsell 4–6–0 class S15 No. 30842, both pointing the 'wrong way' on the two Down lines. The S15 out-dimensions the M7 everywhere except in chimney length. They are framed by the heavy LSWR canopies and awnings which date from the major station re-build of 1900–2. Note the ornate chimneys.

6. The Train in the Countryside

In this chapter, trains are set between quiet meadows, fine trees and in great cuttings. The taking of such pictures can be time-consuming, requiring the climbing of fences, clambering through undergrowth and the ascent of banks to find that perfect viewpoint, often well back from the track. (Only once did an irate farmer chase the author away.) After setting the camera and tripod, the reward is to lie back in the grass, to relax, absorb the country air and write up one's notes while waiting for the train. If the train, sunshine and exhaust then behave as expected, the results can be spectacular – not so much of train detail but of the landscape. An extreme example of such work is a photograph by John Topham (*Reference 5*, p. viii) from the top of Polhill, showing a long trail of steam with the train completely hidden in low morning mist. Another by C.C.B. Herbert shows an LNER train totally dwarfed by West Highland mountains (*Reference 5*, p. viii).

To be honest, having been brought up in the brick and tarmac jungle of South London, it was the discovery of fine countryside which the author enjoyed as much as his pursuit of railway interests. This youthful experience inspired him later in life to walk the open countryside from Land's End to John O'Groats (via Wales, Ireland and the Hebrides), followed by Bristol to the Zuider Zee and then Lancashire to Picardy. But the railway was pursued first – at every opportunity until the end of steam.

Railway artists enjoy countryside settings. They have the advantage of being able to conjure up locomotives and trains from the past, in liveries of their choice. They can also add (or delete) people, animals, structures, vehicles and other ancillaries 'at will'. In the paintings of Ellis, Breckon and Woods, we find cars, buses, vans, lorries, tractors, bikes, tents, rowing-boats, aeroplanes, soldiers, cricketers and a rainbow. We can also find horse, zebra, cattle, sheep, seagull, squirrel, golden eagle, golden oriole, chicken, woodpecker, snake, donkey, grouse, pony, dog, duck, pigeon and one Ellis cat sitting on the line (a forerunner of Terence Cuneo's mouse, perhaps?). In the author's experience, such creatures generally kept well away from trains and photographers. Two notable exceptions are the grazing cows in *Plate 129* and a pair of horses in his previous book, *Odd Corners of the Southern from the Days of Steam*.

Some special terminology appears in this and adjacent chapters, unlikely to be found in general dictionaries. The term 'signalry' encompasses all visible signalling equipment. Terms like townscape, villagescape, railwayscape, skyscape, cloudscape, rainscape and stationscape are specific forms of the general term 'landscape'. The latter is used herein in the artistic sense of 'scenery' rather than in the design sense of 'wider than tall' (although in many cases, both senses apply). Similarly, the term 'portrait' is used in its artistic sense, meaning a close-up (of a person or locomotive) rather than in the design sense of 'taller than wide'. Other terms are defined where they occur.

Rural branch lines dominate this chapter. They were highly photogenic because they were narrow and quaint, and because they were served by a wealth of ancient locomotives and rolling stock. During the final decade of steam, SR branches were havens of pre-Group 0–4–4 tanks, especially Wainwright class H, Drummond class M7 and Adams class O2. The pre-Group coaches were mostly low-roof, their interiors and exteriors bristling with wood and metal fittings. Such longevity is a tribute to the designers and manufacturers of the late nineteenth and early twentieth centuries.

Plate 114: A few miles west of Faversham, a brick road bridge and a clump of silver birch create a thick L-shape composition. They frame a Ramsgate–Victoria train headed by rebuilt 'West Country' class Pacific No. 34001 *Exeter* – first of its class. Shiny Maunsell coaches reflect skylight, but the grimy side of the locomotive remains unilluminated. Cheerful sunlight from the right reflects from the oval smoke-box and the six electric headcode lamps. Billowing smoke is a fine bonus, complementing the birch and seemingly making them yield. Sadly, this was the very last day of steam on the LCDR main line. When the East Kent Railway opened in 1858, locomotion was modest – six 'small Hawthorns' hired from the GNR and then six new 4–4–0 saddle tanks of its own.

Plate 116 (*opposite, below*): A rich Surrey landscape west of Reigate, with a wealth of grasses, bushes and trees, topped by a telegraph pole, an electricity pole and a bank of ragged white cumulus against the blue summer sky. A slightly elevated viewpoint brings out the full beauty of the shallow-angled cutting. Careful timing keeps the mundane train to the middle-distance, apparently 'running through grasses' – always a satisfying and restful impression. Class N Mogul No. 31627 is coasting with just a trace of smoke, its shape caught nicely in the high side-sun. The headcode is an odd mix of Southern discs and a lamp – indicative of the connection of this route with the Western Region at Reading. GWR locos also worked this line, alas not much cleaner than the SR Moguls.

Plate 115: Raised like a signal arm, a branch of cherry makes an unusual feature to frame an Up train near the village of Hoo, at the gentle, cultivated end of the Allhallows line. A windbreak of poplars provides a backcloth while foreground grasses and concrete fence posts obscure the track, with the train apparently riding on air. The train is pre-Group, with SECR class H tank No. 31263 heading two push–pull sets of SECR and LBSCR origin. The driver and cotton-wool steam are bonuses. It was a long train to cater for the August Bank Holiday traffic.

Plate 119: In a picturesque cutting near High Halstow Halt, class H tank No. 31263 hauls a couple of old coaches past an SR distant signal with a broken finial. The cutting, trees and grasses provide an outer frame while the signal and telegraph poles are an inner frame. It is the side-lighting, however, which brings the scene to life, with contrasts of deep shadow and sunlight, just catching the driver and the front of his engine. It would appear that the signal is power-operated, supplied via the short telegraph pole to a motor behind the balance-arm. The picture is an epitome of the remote rural branch line. It was idyllic to walk the single track towards infinity.

Plate 117 (*opposite, above*): Leafless trees in silhouette create an eerie, dramatic framework for a train at speed near the summit of the Oxted line near Woldingham. Weak winter sunlight falls upon the side of the locomotive in a dapple effect, and illuminates the vigorous billows of steam exhaust. Note also the rich texture in the foreground grasses, a sort of glistening glade on the transition from cutting to embankment. The deep shadow of the smokebox heightens the drama, and our eyes drift to the coaches – a mix of Maunsell and Bulleid – refuges of warmth, comfort and repose in this chilly scene. The standard 2–6–4 class 4MT tank is unidentified.

Plate 118 (*opposite, below*): This steep-sided greensand cutting south of Sevenoaks provides a fine setting for a Down boat train headed by a very clean light class Pacific No. 34091 *Weymouth*. The semi-elevated viewpoint shows the train to full advantage, enhanced by the rich backcloth of trees and undergrowth – a haven for wildlife. Other railway detail includes tunnel electrification jumble and a colour-light signal, unique on this section of the Southern, shining directly into Sevenoaks tunnel (see also *Plate 54*). The raised signal arm and sidings (just visible) mark the 1939 limit of electrification. New third rails await installation, laid loosely on the sleepers.

Plate 121: Near Partridge Green, a challenging geometric composition. A low tripod and careful focusing were needed to achieve a Depth of Field from about 6 ft to infinity. The moving train is sharp – the square outline of LSWR class M7 tank No. 30049 at the head of a push–pull set, seemingly 'emerging from grasses'. The red-and-white SR Beware sign is also sharp, leaning back drunkenly on its old-rail post to relieve the squareness of the composition. Together with a bank of foreground grasses and a great silhouetted overhang of scrub oak, they provide a 'telescopic' frame. The leaning crewman is a bonus, but there is no steam or smoke on this occasion.

Plate 120 (*opposite*): In L-shaped compositions, the mind's eye will generally add the two missing sides to complete the frame – try drawing one on a sheet of white paper! This tall portrait is on the tight curve between Groombridge and Ashurst Junction, part of the neat triangle of rural lines in the LBSCR's north-eastern corner. Maunsell push–pull set No. 602 is headed by SECR class H tank No. 31005, moving away and therefore inducing the eye round the curve towards Surrey and north Sussex. The telegraph too, just visible through the exhaust, beckons us on. The great trees on the left, however, provide the substance and majesty of the setting.

Plate 122: A chilly winter's scene in Surrey with the new concrete platforms of Hurst Green Halt in the distance. Weak sunlight percolates the leafless trees to create a dapple effect upon the train. Undergrowth glistens on both sides of the cutting. Oxted's Up distant signal is crystal-clear, providing foreground interest and a visual stop. Together with a fogman's hut and mixed trees, they frame an SECR class H tank with a push–pull set. The lattice signal post and cruciform finial are SR, inherited from the LSWR. The arm looks wire-operated – the insulator by the finial is presumably for the electric lamp. The vigorous plume of grey-white exhaust is a wonderful bonus.

Plate 124 (*opposite, below*): A thick L-shaped composition at Brasted, using a low oak bough for foreground framing. Compared with the end-on panorama in *Plate 104*, the station and train are more elongated in this unusual side-shot. The SER hipped roof and Maunsell's sharp-cornered carriage windows are distinctive, but the locomotive might at first be mistaken for an LSWR tank. It is, of course, the ubiquitous SECR class H, its number 31263 clear and sharp. The leading coach is surprisingly empty, considering that this was the final day of Westerham branch services. The end stations swarmed with enthusiasts, young and old, with posses of wandering photographers. This 5-mile long country branch line was much missed, being easy to visit from the Metropolis.

Plate 123: This L-shaped landscape near Ashey uses a lone winter sycamore for the short vertical side and a combination of field, train and Ashey Down for the long horizontal side. The trail of exhaust steam adds to the horizontalness. Some 50 per cent of the picture is sky, although this is relieved by modest tones of sky-colour. The dark green train of mixed SECR/LBSCR stock is headed by LSWR class O2 tank No. 27 *Merstone*, ambling through the fields towards Smallbrook and Ryde. Track is left to the imagination. Low evening sun reflects from the train side, particularly the ventilator hoods and door handles, creating a 'silver arrow' effect with the leading coaches the focus of attention. The great tree, however, is the geometric 'key' to this composition – try covering it up and the picture becomes quite ordinary. Note the more distant trees (over the loco) which create an 'echo effect'.

Plate 127: Near Overton, an express from Exeter is headed by 'West Country' class Pacific No. 34026 *Yes Tor*. What a wonderful name for an engine, sounding so strong and positive! It is framed by a telegraph pole, an overhang of oak leaves and a wide cutting of summer flowers and grasses – open, wild and free from agriculture.

Plate 125 (*opposite, above*): The Kentish 'Garden of England' with the High Weald beyond, photographed from above the south portal of Sevenoaks tunnel. Floating cotton-wool cumulus provides sky texture and a patchwork of sunshine and shadow upon this grandest of shallow-angled cuttings. An SECR push–pull train, dead-centre, obliges with some steam. The tracks bisect the picture but this 'duality' does not matter from such an elevated viewpoint. Two signals and a hut provide foreground interest, but all are dwarfed by the grand landscape.

Plate 126 (*opposite, below*): SECR class H tank No. 31322 heads a Maunsell push–pull train in the Medway Valley near Wateringbury. The front of the engine stands out sharply against the open landscape beyond. Framing is provided by leafless winter trees, a grassy bank, a Whistle sign, telegraph poles and wires, none of which is dominant. Note also the 'train emerging from cutting' effect, enhanced by the drift of exhaust steam in front of the trees. The eye can meander at leisure, but it should settle upon the engine number-plate and then to the distant valley, enticing one to abandon the railway for a while to explore the river and the oasthouses on the far hill.

Plate 128: A train of flat-sided Maunsell stock approaches Betchworth, headed by a class N Mogul. This summer landscape is divided into three distinct zones: dark trees (top left); the north-facing bank of textured scrub (middle); and the south-facing bank of grasses and flowers (right). The inter-zone dividing lines lead the eye to the station, as does the telegraph and the train moving away from us. Certain details of the country station are discernible, including the Up siding, the level-crossing and a steeply pitched roof – but its character is left mostly to the imagination. In *Reference 6*, p. viii, Axel Brück discusses the forcefulness and dynamism of converging triangles, especially if a long diagonal rises from the bottom-left corner. Its mirror image, on the other hand, with the long diagonal rising from the bottom right, is considered more tranquil and melancholy, as exemplified in *Plate 131*, perhaps. The reasons for this are obscure, hidden deep within the artistic zone of the mind.

Plate 130 (*opposite, below*): A study of light and angularity near Gomshall, featuring a Down train of flat-sided Maunsells headed by SECR class N Mogul No. 31851, making light exhaust. The low camera position and side-light bring out the deep shadow of the right-hand bank (a 45° isosceles triangle), together with great trees in silhouette. This contrasts with the sunny far bank, studded with smaller trees, bushes and telegraph poles. Triangles of sky and cutting, together with the tracks and train, all converge towards infinity. A cover photo by Edward Griffith (*Reference 2*, p. viii) makes similar use of trees and shadow but with an LSWR train on the Meon Valley line.

Plate 129: Against a sky of cobalt blue, a clean SECR class H tank No. 31278 produces a splendid trail of safety-valve steam near Edenbridge Town. During the latter days of steam, most trains on the Oxted–Hever–Tunbridge Wells West service were push-pull, but it was rare to find a 'birdcage' set. The SECR discontinued such stock in 1915. The setting too is unusual – a field of Jersey cows, their shadows and a railway fence, with the train 'emerging from conifers'. The white wooden structure looks like a toppled speed-restriction sign.

Plate 131: The High Weald of East Sussex was once topped by the dense forest of Andredesweald. Clusters of trees remain, as seen at St Margaret's junction. LBSCR 0–6–0 class C2X No. 32521 'runs light' off the start of the Bluebell line while the signalman chats to another railwayman by the spur to East Grinstead high-level. The vintage locomotive is

framed by trees, grassy banks, a signal, telegraph poles, the Saxby & Farmer signal-box and a concrete hut (which looks like a closet). The elevated viewpoint opens up the landscape to full advantage, with some nice shadow effects on the left. Note the four point rods – 'operating' and 'lock' for each junction point.

Plate 132: Only the lightest of locomotives were permitted to cross the wooden viaduct to Hayling Island, but there was no restriction on coaches. Photographers too were constrained regarding variety of composition, on account of the openness of the Hayling countryside. One solution was to stand well back from the line, using a framework of scrub oak or hawthorn to depict the tiny 'Terrier' tanks pulling heavy trains. Such was the case at the northern end of the island, beneath a cloud-dappled sky. One BR and two SR coaches are headed by No. 32650, formerly No. 50 *Whitechapel* – the name of an Underground station once served by the LBSCR.

Plate 134: There is much nostalgia for the mainland class O2 tanks, since none is preserved. No. 30236 is photographed head-on at Nanstallon Halt, departing with a short train of Maunsells for Bodmin North. A glimpse of concrete platform, tall signals, squat signal-box and a crossing-keeper's house provides additional interest, but this is primarily a landscape – a small train in the rich setting of the Camel Valley. Using side-light and a thick L-shaped frame, it is a strong composition, enhanced by the distant dome of moorland. After taking in the scene, the track curvature returns us to the point of focus – the white house. This line today is the Camel Cycleway.

Plate 133 (*opposite, below*): As one stands further and further back from the lineside, trains are in danger of disappearing completely in the landscape. Scenery must be special to justify such pictures. These winter sycamores near Ashey are exceptional for their shiny trunks, tortuous boughs and overall diamond-shapes. Framing is completed by the white fence posts and brick road bridge, obscuring all but two of the coaches. The train's presence and progress are announced by the trailing exhaust steam. The cleanliness of the locomotive helps us to focus upon it – class O2 No. 25 *Godshill* – *en route* to Newport and Cowes. If the trees still exist, this picture might well be repeated today, for it is near the eastern end of the preserved Isle of Wight Steam Railway.

Plate 135: At Horam, after battling through undergrowth, the result was this idyllic setting from a bank of Scots pine. The station has shrunk to model-railway proportions but a gentle puff of steam confirms that it is real. The raised SR signal arm helps to set the scene in motion, endorsed by the Southdown bus crossing the bridge. This landscape or 'villagescape' has glimpses of houses amidst trees, served not only by a fine-looking station but by the goods yard and coal wagons (both wooden and steel). The U-shaped framing uses curtains of pine and a carpet of shrub to emphasize the beauty of man's achievements here. LMS Fairburn 2–6–4 tank No. 42087 heads two utility vans and three coaches, all SR Maunsell, bound for Eastbourne. It is a scene of contentment.

Plate 136: For variety, the author crossed the Medway south of Teston Crossing. Ripples precluded clear reflections, but the landscapes were rewarding. This train is bound for Maidstone West – an SECR class H tank heading a bright set of BR Mark 1 coaches in crimson and cream – an uncommon livery on the Southern Region. It brings life to a skyline of leafless winter trees, spreading cedars and roof-tops. The ripples bring life to the river – one can almost see the fish rising. The reflected stump is a visual stop. The incline of the river bank (rising from the right) breaks up the rectangularity and adds to the tranquillity.

Plate 137: Charles Dickens described the eastern end of the Hoo peninsula as flat, bleak, marshy and treeless. In the days of steam, it presented a challenge for creative photography. On an overcast winter day, one solution was to retreat on to the marshes and to use this ramshackle gate, ditch and grass for foreground interest, together with the Isle of Grain oil refinery on the skyline. They frame a push–pull train broadside-on in silhouette, enhanced by a long trail of steam and sky colour. The resulting landscape is dramatic, made all the more so by the use of a 'hard' paper in the darkroom, ensuring rich texture for the foreground but producing a grainy image overall.

7. Smoke, Steam and Sky

Steam locomotives have the special feature of mixing steam exhaust with the gases of combustion. With the regulator valve open, steam passes from the cylinders to 'blast pipes' at the base of the chimney to create a vacuum, known as the 'venturi effect'. This 'draws' flue gases from the firebox, in turn drawing fresh air through the grate and dampers below. With the regulator closed, air-flow over the chimney also 'draws' the fire in a weaker suction effect. When stationary, the 'blower' valve can be opened to pass 'live steam' direct from the boiler to the chimney. When cold, the fire must rely upon natural draught or be assisted by a portable fan.

For any given fuel, there is an 'ideal' air quantity which just completes combustion of carbon, hydrogen and sulphur. In practice, the molecules do not mix intimately, so 'excess air' is needed for complete combustion. With too much 'excess air', the fire overheats and energy is wasted in chimney gases. Incandescent grits, known as 'sparks', can also be carried through, with risk of lineside fires. Too little 'excess air', on the other hand, produces unburnt carbon, both as solid 'grits' and as gaseous hydrocarbons. This mix, called smoke, is largely avoidable by careful firing and damper-setting. When stoking or wheel-slipping, however, some smoke is unavoidable for short periods, producing dramatic effects. The photographer must be ready for such occasions.

Steam exhaust is more predictable than smoke – especially on inclines or during station starts and if the air is cool. During icy weather, the trail of steam can be exceptionally long. The photographer must be wary of possible obscuration of the train by steam, either directly or from its shadow. Sun direction is another factor, with side-light bringing out multiple tones of colour in the billows of exhaust. Blue sky can be darkened with a yellow filter, to emphasize exhaust and cloud. The latter are constantly changing but can enrich train pictures to produce some fine 'skyscapes'. Of the ten common categories of cloud, the most interesting pictorially are as follows:

Cirrus cloud is ice particles at the highest altitudes. It is thin, delicate, white, fibrous, sometimes silky, usually with tufts or feathery plumes – see *Plates 21, 28, **110**, 184*.

Cirrocumulus (lower than cirrus) comprises small white flakes or globules of ice, arranged in lines or ripples, often called a 'mackerel sky' – see *Plates 10, **157***.

Stratocumulus has layers, globular masses or rolls of water vapour, soft and white-grey, sometimes in regular rows – see *Plates 6, 30, 80, 84, 118, 138, **159**, 160, 161, 170*.

Cumulus are individuals (lower than stratocumulus). They have a domed top and near-horizontal base, often arranged in regular patterns. When viewed up-sun, the edges are bright, known as the 'silver lining' – see *Plates 20, 32, 35, 125, 132, **158**, 162, **164***.

Stratus is a grey, uniform, often continuous layer of low cloud, sometimes with breaks, commonly called 'overcast' – see *Plates 13, 33, **39**, 98, 99, 109, 144, 163, 171*.

Cumulonimbus are great vertical storm clouds. *Plate 179* is beneath an April shower.

Plate 138 (*opposite*): A busy scene at Havant where railwaymen outnumber passengers. A fireman appears to be operating the blower valve, hence the tall column of smoke which semi-obscures the sky and forms the upright of a thick L-shaped composition. The focus of attention is LBSCR 'Terrier' tank No. 32661, looking small but stately at the front of a train of Maunsell stock. The spark-arrestor on the chimney is a precaution against fire on the Hayling viaduct. Note the long lamp-irons, the SR trolley with train lamps and an assortment of garden sheds.

Plate 141: When R.E.L.Maunsell's 'Lord Nelson' class was introduced in 1926, they should have been the most powerful locomotives on Britain's railways. Although not the most successful of 4–6–0s, they were exceedingly handsome and much admired. A sleek appearance derived from a long boiler with a 'heavy' front end of long smoke-deflectors and a large-diameter chimney (added by Bulleid from 1938). The narrow angle of the pointed, panther-like spectacle is echoed in both the firebox and the rave of the tender. Approaching Surbiton with a Down boat train to Southampton, No. 30851 *Sir Francis Drake* issues carbon-rich billows of smoke, no doubt during stoking. The train is framed by the trees, a road bridge, a retaining wall (right), sand and ballast bins and two Limit of Shunt signs. C. Hamilton Ellis used a similar setting near Surbiton for one of his colourful paintings (*Reference 2*, p. viii), showing a Drummond T9 overtaking an Adams 'radial' tank, both on Down trains, with an open-top tram on the bridge. This grand cutting was always photogenic, but it is *Sir Francis* who steals the show here.

Plate 139 (*opposite, above*): Double-heading was commonplace for the heavier trains on the Evercreech to Bath section of the Somerset & Dorset line. Approaching Windsor Hill tunnel, 'West Country' class Pacific No. 34028 *Eddystone* is piloted by standard class 5MT No. 73024, making a heavy pall of smoke which drifts down over the train from Bournemouth. The locomotives too are grimy, leaving an impression of wanton pollution against the neat fields to either side. The composition uses trees, fences and the telegraph for framing, enhanced by the diverging tracks. The sinister-looking platelayers' hut, with its re-pointed chimney, bisects the running lines in what was once a cutting-side of the original single track. This unusual setting can also be studied in *Plate 55*.

Plate 140 (*opposite, below*): Standard 4–6–0 class 5 No. 73113 slips its wheels as it re-starts from Whitchurch North with a smart train of Bulleid stock, bound for Salisbury. The spectacular result is a great column of smoke, neatly bisecting the composition. Unstable 'duality' is avoided by the visual strength of the right-hand side – comprising the side-drift of smoke, the long black-and-white shed and the old sleepers stacked upright against the bank. Other railway interest includes the pointwork, telegraph, SR platelayers' hut, the curved canopy of the island platform and a lattice footbridge to the station building – brick-built with a hipped roof. Steam below the injector was a bonus to enhance this powerful action picture. One can almost hear the staccato bark of exhaust.

Plate 142: A powerful impression in silhouette of LSWR class M7 tank No. 30051, gathering speed with a three-coach push–pull set north of Baynards. In a rich setting of undergrowth and trees, a sense of power is imparted by three elements: first, the up-sun aspect which brings out every billow of the great exhaust (you can count the last six blasts); second, the square framework of the signal and the cruciform telegraph pole; and third, the squareness of the train itself – from the buffer-beam and leading sand boxes to the flat sides of the water tank, cab and leading SECR coach. The low wisps of steam are a softening bonus. New concrete sleepers contrast with the discarded wooden ones. The tapered wooden signal post is LBSCR with an SR fixed-distant steel arm.

Plate 144 (*opposite, below*): At Blandford Forum, a busy composition packed with railway interest. Centre-stage, a grimy standard class 5 No. 73047 re-starts a north-bound train with an intense column of smoke. This is softened to some extent by wisps of steam below, to the right and from the train on the left. Another central feature is the intriguing outline of the water-column – an inverted U with top-support and a self-centring wheel. In the loop platform, GWR Pannier tank No. 4691 marshals a mixed goods train. Foreground detail includes a point-lever, shunting disc, trailing point and point-rod boarding. Framing is completed by the left-hand huts, S&D signal-box and the rear of a Bulleid coach. This low viewpoint misses the townscape but brings out the smoke to the full.

Plate 143: On the long curve south of Ryde, a class O2 tank heads a five-coacher with two LBSCR low-arc-roof coaches at the front. There is no scope for passenger confusion with this train, for No. 16 *Ventnor* is indeed bound for Ventnor! From an elevated viewpoint and with weak sunlight reflecting off the train side, the framework should have comprised the white gate (right), fences, grasses and a long skyline of trees and buildings (the outskirts of Ryde). The fireman, however, had other ideas and provided instead this magnificent trail of smoky exhaust, looking much too energetic for such a diminutive locomotive. The days of steam were not clean!

Plate 146: The LMS Ivatt 2–6–2 tanks give a hearty bark when they start. At Watergate Halt, on the remote china-clay line south of Torrington, violent exhaust echoes between the conifers as No. 41295 departs southwards with a single Bulleid brake-third, emerging through a halo of cylinder drain steam. Note how the side-lighting catches the wheels and ladder. A sunlit foreground of telegraph pole, fence posts and bushes contrasts with the massive backcloth of dark, foreboding trees. A short SR concrete platform is hidden by the train. In a similar composition here from an earlier era, George Heiron painted an LBSCR/SR class E1/R tank with a single LSWR coach (*Reference 3*, p. viii, May 1961, interpreted from a photograph by Anne Carter). Both Heiron and *Plate 146* include the half-face of a driver and emphasize the smallness of the train in deep forest. But it is the power of the steam and smoke which dominate here – a triumph of thermodynamic engineering over nature.

Plate 145 (*opposite*): This L-shaped composition at Sandown uses a tall column of exhaust with trees, the train and platform with its great canopy and elevated signal-box. On a still, cool morning, the silhouetted steam has a slight drift as class O2 tank No. 28 *Ashey* re-starts a train to Ventnor. The Westinghouse air-brake pump stands out clearly on the front. The buffer-stop (left) was a recent addition to the loop platform, once the start of the Isle of Wight Central line to Newport. The discarded sleepers and rails are probably from the former loop points.

Plate 147: The wide, open spaces of Ashford provide a perfect setting to depict steam trains re-starting from the Down platform. On a still winter's morning, SECR class L No. 31781 obliges with a fine plume of exhaust steam and some open cylinder-cocks. This was Harry Wainwright's heaviest class of 4–4–0 express engine. Note the wide splashers, the rear one merging with the cab. No. 781 was the last of a batch built by Borsig of Berlin and handed over to the SECR on the opening day of the First World War. It heads a train of Bulleid stock destined for the Canterbury West line to Margate. The Maunsell stock (right) provide counterpoint. Framing is completed by the great SECR 'albatross' canopy with deep awning. It is the steam, however, which brings everything to life.

Plate 148 (*opposite*): The Drummond 0–4–4 class M7 tanks were privileged with low BR(S) numbering. LSWR No. 49 is captured re-starting from Cranleigh with an early train to Horsham. In the still, cool air, not long after dawn, steam rises high, not only from the exhaust but from the blowing safety-valve. Photographed three-quarters into the sun, all shades of grey are evident in the violent steam effect. Silhouetted or in shadow, there is a rich framework of trees, the leading coach, a neat platform and signals. The whitened platform edge leads us along the gentle curve of the track to the wooded countryside beyond. The tall SR Home signal and leaning telegraph pole resemble a distant gateway. The foreground starter and shunting arm are SR, mounted upon a squat, square LBSCR post with unsharp finial. The open window of the SECR coach is an warm invitation to go for a trip.

Plate 149: Near Yalding, low evening sunlight brings out texture in a triangle of foreground grasses which occupy some 40 per cent of this Medway Valley landscape. Taking care with the tripod position and Depth of Field setting, a small forest of Trespassing, other signs, signals and posts is used for framing. They were originally intended for a train approaching the camera, but this set of BR Mark 1s passed in the Maidstone direction, casting a long trail of exhaust steam which was irresistible. Everything is sharp. The rear lamp bids a 'farewell'.

Plate 151: A contrast of soft steam and strong signalry at Ashford. Blowing off, draining cylinders and creating a most energetic show of vapour and noise, standard class 4MT tank No. 80085 is cloaked in its own effects in the yard behind the Hastings bay. All that is missing is the emergence of Robbie's father at the end of the film *The Railway Children*. Solid reference points are provided by the platform, distant pointwork and silhouetted signalry – gantry, cantilever, doll, cruciform spiked finial, part of an arm, a shunting disc, railings and an SR mechanical route indicator – resembling a black tunnel in the sky. A new power signal-box is under construction beyond.

Plate 150 (*opposite, below*): On a cloudless, blue-skied, icy morning, this drift of exhaust steam has the magnitude of a power station cooling tower plume, seemingly changing the climate around Tonbridge. The culprit is an unidentified SECR 0–6–0 class C, shunting a BR parcels van on to the rear of a Down train. The locomotive, barely visible, is the focus of attention. It is framed by a wealth of detail from the SR Maunsell era (1923–37) which includes a van, coaches, signals, lamps, trolleys and a concrete name-sign. The strength of the composition derives from the long diagonal of drifting steam which combines with the platforms and tracks to create triangles which converge at the signal-box. Key visual stops are the utility van (right), the group of people, a skyline of signalry and two sets of hexagonal lamps on art-deco arms. The enamelled '6' is for short Hastings DMUs, shortly to be used also by EMUs.

Plate 153: According to Vera Lynn, *There'll be bluebirds over the White Cliffs of Dover*. Below them, however, there'll be a post-war 'Golden Arrow' of Pullman stock, headed by rebuilt heavy Pacific No. 35015 *Rotterdam Lloyd*, accelerating towards Shakespeare Cliff tunnel with a fine display of exhaust steam. The strong cliff-diagonal continues through to the siding on the right. The composition is made more powerful and dramatic by the low viewpoint, with the train bearing down upon the camera. The locomotive looks immaculate, with skylight reflected from its side. Low evening sun catches the 'GA' insignia perfectly, with shadows playing upon the silver oval around the smoke-box door. Three 'Merchant Navy's were allocated to Stewarts Lane for such duty.

Plate 152 (*opposite*): The class N Mogul was a utility mixed-traffic workhorse which was introduced by the SECR in 1917. In many ways plain-looking, they performed well until the end of steam. No. 31826 is swathed in steam of its own making as it re-starts a train from the Down platform at Tonbridge. Cylinder cocks are open and the safety valve is blowing, but it is the majestic plume of exhaust steam which captures our attention, with delicate shades of grey caught in the cross-light of the low morning sun. Taken three-quarters up-sun, the dirty side of the locomotive just about manages a reflection. The bridge, canopy, cab, water-column and tracks, however, remain mostly in deep shadow, heightening the drama of the scene. The head of steam is never in doubt!

Plate 156: The LSWR 4–6–0 class S15 was more powerful and more simple-looking than its Ashford mixed-traffic contemporaries on the opposite page. All three classes were developed by Maunsell to their final SR versions. No. 30499 is a Urie original, however, producing a long trail of billowing exhaust in the wide open spaces west of Basingstoke. The coaches are BR Mark 1s except for a Pullman towards the rear – running empty to Eastleigh, perhaps? Framing is provided by fences, trees, telegraph poles, grasses and spring flowers. The five-track main line makes a particularly strong diagonal, creating a collection of soft triangles which converge towards infinity, just beyond the trees. This engine was a delight after a procession of Bulleid Pacifics.

Plate 154 (*opposite, above*): A grimy class N Mogul No. 31851 climbs between Tonbridge and High Brooms with a train of flat-sided Maunsell stock bound for Eridge, Lewes and Brighton. Woodland of silver birch provides a winter backcloth, balanced by the scrub, telegraph pole and wires on the left. The picture is 'made', however, by the long trail of exhaust steam, drifting up and over the telegraph and framing the train. Without the steam, the picture would be somewhat grey, flat and unexciting. The two vans suggest that this was a key mail service.

Plate 155 (*opposite, below*): What a difference a cleaning-rag makes! This Continental freight train is photographed near Smeeth on the SER main line to Folkestone (note the motor-car exports). Compared with *Plate 154*, the locomotive looks immaculate, every rivet gleaming on the cylinder housings above the buffer-beam. Class U1 Mogul No. 31908 was built in 1931, a three-cylinder tender variation of Maunsells' ill-fated class K 2–6–4 tanks. It is framed here by the telegraph, grasses, leafless shrubs and the magnificent plume of its own exhaust.

Plate 157: Rich velvety sky effects can be achieved by using a yellow filter on the camera and a 'soft' paper in the darkroom. This striking composition on Norden Heath comprises 75 per cent 'mackerel' sky, 20 per cent heath and 5 per cent train. A class M7 tank propels a Maunsell push–pull set towards Swanage. Note the deep, up-sun shadow throughout.

Plate 158: Flotillas of perfectly-cloned 'floating' cumulus are a phenomenon special to south-east England, tending to evaporate to nothing within hours (see also *Plate 125*). Here at Dorking Town, they dominate the sky and blend well with the vertical exhaust plume of a grey-looking class N Mogul No. 31863 on a train to Guildford. Ground-level interest is provided by the signals, telegraph, goods shed, wagon, SER signal-box and station building.

Plate 161: Near Glastonbury, a bright broken 'cloudscape' in John Constable proportions (60 per cent of the picture), making even the drift of exhaust look dark and subsidiary. The Somerset Levels are challenging for railway photography, but by crossing the ditch to a more distant viewpoint, this grassy embankment emerges, enhanced by some scattered trees and a wooden signal post which is probably of S&D vintage. The Western Region train is headed by a Collett 0–6–0, the only SR representative being the Maunsell utility van at the rear. One is left in awe of the builders of this remote, watery line with its formidable foundations and modest traffic prospects.

Plate 159 (*opposite, above*): Sky occupies 50 per cent of this landscape at Edenbridge Town – broken stratocumulus tinged with bright edges, carefully exposed in the darkroom. The setting is a wide, shallow cutting, framed by houses, a vegetable patch, leafless oak trees and goods yard staithes. We focus upon the train – class H tank No. 31518 propelling a push–pull set to Oxted. Encouraged by a hazy trail of exhaust and the long line of the telegraph, our eyes ride the Maunsell coaches past the SER goods shed, through the Up platform and into the verdant plain beyond. An elevated viewpoint makes all this possible. This was a delightful double-track, double-ended branch.

Plate 160 (*opposite, below*): A bank of creamy cumulus brings a colourful finish to this summer scene by the River Camel just east of Wadebridge. A grey class N Mogul No. 31844 heads a train of green Bulleid stock up the North Cornwall line towards Exeter. The elevated viewpoint brings out the estuary, the country lane, a row of terraced cottages and the rooftops of the town. In his long poem *Cornwall in Childhood*, John Betjeman recalls the delights of reaching this location by train (*Reference 4*, p. viii). He is amazed to have travelled in the same carriage from Waterloo, and he relishes the scent of Cornish air and the 'silence after steam' upon arrival at Wadebridge station. Here the train is moving with full noise, indicated by the drift of white exhaust below the summer clouds.

Plate 162: At the start of the single-track 'Cuckoo' line, just west of Polegate, a standard 2–6–4 class 4MT tank produces a fine display of steam at the head of a train of flat-sided Maunsell stock. Vagaries of breeze distort the exhaust into grotesque form, standing out against the white-tinged cumulus above and beyond. The tight curve facilitates this window-leaning viewpoint which also brings out the loading dock and horse-box. Framing is completed by the coaches, grasses, shrubs, water-tower and hipped domestic roofs in 1930s' style. Note also the check-rail and the array of point-rodding (bottom right). But this is primarily a study of water vapour displays.

Plate 164 (*opposite, below*): Up-sun photographs can be dramatic, with contrasts of deep shadow and light, and some spectacular cloud effects. This example at Gomshall and Shere has all of this as well as a complex framework of barrows, name-sign, gas lamps, some far signals, staggered platforms, a wooden shelter, lamp room, passenger-crossing and telegraph pole – mostly in silhouette. They frame a freight train in the middle-distance, headed by a Bulleid 0–6–0 class Q1 with its unmistakable horse-shoe of a smoke-box. The composition invites one to walk the platforms and to bask in the glory of the last days of steam. A notebook was held up to shade the camera lens. The cumulus is delicately scattered, with flimsy linings and strong back-lighting to produce 'heavenly radiance'.

Plate 163: Taken from the LSWR mainline platforms, this broadside at Clapham Junction brings out the handsome features of a standard 2–6–4 tank of which ninety-three were built at Brighton from 1951. No. 80151 re-starts an Oxted train of SR Maunsell stock on the climb to Victoria. The proportions of boiler, cylinder, valve gear, side-tank, cab and bunker look perfect, enhanced by the illuminated face of the driver and several wisps of steam. Lighting is ideal, with the low evening sun reflected from the locomotive side and leading coach to create a 'silver arrow' effect (see also *Plate 123*). Horizontalness is confirmed by the foreground rails and streaks of grey in the banks of overcast sky beyond. Evening sunlight can have great luminosity which is apparent here.

8. Other Compositions

This final chapter is devoted to types of composition not specifically covered in the earlier chapters. They are: high and low viewpoints; trains as frames; window-leaning; up-sun pictures; some pure 'railwayscapes'; trains with buildings; trains moving away; a 'rainscape'; engine shed interiors; foreground signs; and a bow-shot. They further illustrate the rich variety of compositions that can be discovered with a creative eye, in contrast to the stereotypic approach of purely 'record' photography.

What can be learnt from the pictures in this book? The author has learnt a great deal, feeling obliged to examine critically every composition for artistic merit and technical detail. Like a visit to an art gallery, it requires discipline and time to examine pictures properly – also patience, waiting for those magic moments of appreciation which emerge from the inner mind. Some pictures have so much impact that they are instantly appreciated. Others are more complex or subtle, requiring time to discover their hidden values. A few are puzzling or unstable, keeping the viewers on their toes!

On the locomotive front, the fleet herein is a fair cross-section of the classes encountered by the author and a reasonable representation of the locomotive population during the final decade of steam. Any bias reflects the author's tastes, spare time and bank balance in choosing which lines to visit. The Index at the rear shows twenty-seven classes of tender engine, eighteen classes of tank and two of diesel. Bulleid Pacifics (collectively) are the most numerous, followed by the class H tanks and the standard class 4MT tanks. The ubiquitous class N Mogul is surprisingly in fifth place, just behind the Island O2s and just ahead of the M7 tanks. Of the rarer tank engines, the Stroudley 'Terriers' have a representation out of proportion to their numbers, but the Adams 'radials' and Beattie 'well-tanks' are in better proportion. The LBSCR population as a whole is probably the best loved by the author. Other favourites are the 4–4–0s, the older 4–6–0s, any 2–6–4 tank from the front and any clean Bulleid Pacific.

What has been learnt about composition? The fundamental message is that the best collections of pictures incorporate a wide variety of styles and framing matter. These cannot be determined in advance but must be discovered, station by station and chain by chain along the line. An artistic 'eye' must be developed to sense exactly where to set up the camera so as to include not only a fine train but those vital interesting peripheral items which transform an operational record into a composition of merit to stir the soul. Some attempts will fail, but many will succeed over a period of time. The underlying motivation is a desire to portray the steam railway as a whole, deriving from a love of steam locomotion and its associated infrastructure.

Is there any favourite shape of picture? Some argue squareness to be the most harmonious (*Plates 179, 184*). Others argue for the Golden Rectangle which has sides in the proportion 5:8 (*Plates 174, 176*). This ratio has the magic mathematical relationship a:b = b:(a+b) which is supposed to be the most satisfying to the inner mind. Do you have any preference? The view of Axel Brück (*Reference 7*, p. viii) is that shape is important only for *unfilled* frames, as in classical architecture. Photography, on the other hand, uses frames which are *filled* with interesting subject matter and internal shapes. The conclusion is that external shape matters little. Indeed, the best collections of pictures have a range of shapes. As with the subject matter, variety is the spice of life!

Plate 165: An 'overview' taken by the east portal of Black Boy Road tunnel. It portrays the front and top of the 'Atlantic Coast Express', coasting down the grade to Exeter Central. Detail of light Pacific No. 34034 *Honiton* includes a haze of gaseous exhaust, a simmering safety valve and a well-depleted coal bunker, while the Bulleid coaches show their roof-tanks, filling pipes and ventilators. Elevation also brings out the texture of the grasses and a long sky-line of Exmouth junction's concrete works, marshalling yard and 'Cenotaph' coaling tower.

Plate 166: An elevated, directly up-sun 'stationscape' at Whitchurch North, featuring rebuilt light Pacific No. 34082 *615 Squadron*, running light towards Basingstoke with a light haze of exhaust. This Hurricane squadron, based at Kenley, is still commemorated some sixty years after the Battle of Britain. The evening sun reflects off every running rail, as well as from the locomotive and coals in the foreground wagons. The entire layout is clear; to transfer a wagon to or from the loading dock, the locomotive would leave the local goods train in the loop platform and then reverse via the Up line, Down line and siding. Note the barrow crossing, greatly extended because of the semi-stagger of the platforms. See *Plate 140* for a more conventional view of the same station.

Plate 168 (*opposite, below*): An elevated shot from Lucas Terrace Halt, featuring a train of empty SR stock coasting to Plymouth Friary, the LSWR terminus which closed to passengers in 1958. This three-quarters view shows that SR Pacific No. 34023 *Blackmoor Vale* is clean but has lost its 'West Country' insignia below the name-plate. As with other elevated shots, the landscape opens up, showing the Turnchapel branch (right), a distant River Plym, football fields, the edge of town and a local road with a black-and-white lamp-post – a relic of the wartime blackout. The driver leans out at ease. This is a peaceful scene compared with the drama of *Plates 166* and *167*.

Plate 167: A low viewpoint can produce perspective of great impact. This can be all the more dramatic if taken up-sun, particularly with the front of the train in silhouette and producing a great display of exhaust. The latter was unlikely near Wye when a Bo-Bo class 2 diesel-electric turned up 'on trial' with a set of Bulleids, shortly before electrification. Spanning a transition from cutting to embankment, the locomotive stands out with 3-D effect against a creamy sky. A strong track diagonal passes through the ballast bin. The telegraph pole provides a visual stop, as does the skyline of winter trees. The walking lengthsman is fortuitous – a commendable feature often added by artists like Chris Woods (*Reference 9*, p. viii) and George Heiron (*Reference 3*, p. viii, Nov. 1962). Our eyes return, however, to the rich texture of foreground grasses and the notchy, grainy timber of the bin and old sleepers.

Plate 169: A full 'railwayscape' taken from a footbridge just east of Faversham junction. The elevated viewpoint opens up the scene, inviting us to explore the yards to either side of the Thanet line. A marshalling yard (right) displays assorted open wagons and brake vans while the loco yard (left) holds two Ivatt 2–6–2 tanks, an SR Mogul and a

Wainwright 0–6–0. Centre-stage is a train of pure Maunsell origin, headed by class N Mogul No. 31861. Note the pointwork, yard debris and a new EMU (top left) awaiting E-day. The skyline of trees includes a fine stone church with steeple. A much taller steeple features in Chris Woods' *Sunday at Salisbury* (*Reference 9*, p. viii).

Plate 172: An example of 'framing by rolling stock', taken at Ventnor, the southern terminus of the Isle of Wight Railway. The buffer-stop and run-round loop confirm the location, with class O2 tank No. 31 *Chale* taking water, the centre-piece of the composition. The panelled coaches are LBSCR, identifiable by the long, slender hand-rails. Framing is completed by the bank of bushes and trees, silhouetted against the bright evening sky. Taken almost up-sun, leaning from a window, the light reflects beautifully from the clean loco and far coach.

Plate 170 (*opposite, above*): This 'railwayscape' at Wimbledon incorporates rolling stock, summer clouds and a signal-box perspective to frame a Down Bournemouth express headed by standard 4–6–0 class 4MT No. 75079. The grey front of the steam train is subsidiary to the intriguing shapes all around: flared and clerestoried District Line stock; the sleek, brick, late-SR signal-box with its roof overhang; great ragged cumulus; and the three-rail pointwork.

Plate 171 (*opposite, below*): Beneath a stormy sky, this 'railwayscape' by Dover Marine features a massive backdrop of the White Cliffs, army barracks on the Western Heights and a warehouse and crane in the Western Docks. A closer framework is provided by the low wall (right), an SR signal gantry and the LCDR's former Dover Harbour Station wall (left). Centre-scene is the 'Man of Kent', a fine train of BR Mark 1 stock headed by rebuilt light Pacific No. 34014 *Budleigh Salterton*, *en route* from Margate to Charing Cross via Deal, Ashford and Tonbridge.

Plate 173: Window-leaning at Lewisham Road, using Bulleid coach sides and three-storied Victorian houses for framing. The train to Ramsgate is headed by light Pacific No. 34025 *Whimple*, diverted via the Dartford Loop due to modernization work on the LCDR main line. Our eyes follow it to Parks Bridge which crosses the SER main line, site of the St Johns accident in 1957. Other detail includes check-rails, chimney-pots, trees in blossom, curved walls and grasses by the end of the old station which closed in 1917 along with the Greenwich Park branch.

Plate 174 (*opposite, above*): The Wenford Bridge branch runs on a causeway past the upper storey of this stone cottage near Dunmere. A train of loaded china clay wagons is headed by a Beattie 2–4–0 well-tank. The LSWR introduced this class in 1862 for suburban passenger duty. No. 30585 is preserved on the Buckinghamshire Railway but it is subsidiary here to the house, grasses and rich Cornish landscape. The Bodmin & Wenford Railway currently runs preserved steam trains as far as Boscarne Junction, with prospects of line extensions.

Plate 175 (*opposite, below*): On the Northam curve in Southampton's working-class suburbs, a sinister house of Hitchcock proportions frames a train from Weymouth, headed by 'West Country' class Pacific No. 34098 *Templecombe*. Framing is completed by the far jumble of houses, the cabbage patch (left) and the neglected garden (right). There is much else to explore – the line of washing, the garden out-buildings, the great hoardings for companies of old and Knight's Foot Clinic. We focus upon the loco, but it is a small part of this 'townscape'.

Plate 178: A further example of coach-leaning, with the nearest coach occupying a third of the frame, balanced by the mass of trees and bushes on the right. Good timing was paramount for this up-sun picture – too late and the sun would shine into the lens – too soon and the lighting effects would not be captured. Low evening sunlight reflects strongly from the train side and rails, also illuminating the plume of a class N Mogul, labouring up Sole Street bank from Rochester. The *coup de grâce* is the reflected image in the flat window of the Maunsell coach.

Plate 176 (*opposite, above*): Trains moving away from the camera lead the eye along the intended route. Ivatt 2–6–2 No. 41260 fulfils this function at the head of a Down train at Ashurst, along one of the finest shallow-angled cuttings on the Southern. Framing is provided by the leading brake-composite, a neat platform, bushes, the bank of scattered trees and an inclined road bridge. Note the fine pointwork and reflections in the flat Maunsell windows. The grand landscape competes for our attention, but we always return to the crewman and his imminent journey.

Plate 177 (*opposite, below*): The LMS 2–6–2 tanks look their best when viewed from the front. No. 41242 obliges at Sturminster Newton, leading us northwards (bunker-first) into classic Thomas Hardy country. The GWR coach provides a side-frame, balanced by the signals, point-rodding, far trees and the grey outline of a distant hill. We are invited to climb aboard for a ride to the next station and village which we know instinctively to exist at the base of the hill. The SR starting signalry includes a short semaphore shunting arm – white with red stripes.

Plate 179: Railway 'rainscapes' are rare. Caught in a heavy downpour, Bulleid 0–6–0 class Q1 No. 33037 grinds to a halt at Canterbury East on a passenger train to Dover – a further example of bizarre locomotive duties during the latter days of steam (see *Plates 72* and *167*). Water gushes from the tender and coach gutters. Platform puddles reflect the sky and the unique LCDR signal-box – elevated on steel stilts. This was a careful composition, using a long row of ancient gas lamps for the right-hand framing. Our eyes follow the direction of the train beneath the cantilevered signals, past a two-car EMU (awaiting E-day) and under the distant footbridge to the infinite murk beyond. The scene has much 'atmosphere', evoking fond memories of LCDR main line steam.

Plate 180 (*opposite*): At Chatham, a final tribute to the LCDR, featuring standard 4–6–0 class 4MT No. 75066 on a Down train. There are three 'telescopic' levels of heavy framing – the dark canopy and high-rave tender, the tall road bridge with brick support column, and a tunnel entrance just visible through the murk. Other detail includes the gas lamp, ornate iron bracket, enamelled EMU stop signs, new colour-light signals, a discarded 'not in operation' cross, a track-circuit diamond, hatched telephone box and a pile of debris. The portrait is balanced, the tones are Rembrandtesque, the content is 100 per cent railway. The wonder of Chatham station is that it existed at all, wedged in a short section between two tunnels, an arrangement more characteristic of the District Line.

Plate 181: At Wadebridge MPD, a final tribute to the LSWR, featuring Beattie well-tank No. 30586 and an unidentified Drummond 4–4–0 class T9 (not to be moved!) with its great tender. Relying upon natural lighting, every detail is clear on the ancient 2–4–0, including rivets, springs, 'motion', brake mechanism, sand boxes, side tank and boiler fittings. Note also the wooden roof trusses, smoke extraction ducts, wooden wall, grossly inadequate SR lamps and the greasy, watery floor by the inspection pit. It was a modest shed of great character.

Plate 182 (*opposite, above*): At Fratton MPD, a final tribute to the SR, featuring Maunsell class U Mogul No. 31807 (rebuilt in the late 1920s from SECR class K tank No. 807 *River Axe*). This joint LSWR/LBSCR shed was a roundhouse of steel and brick, much larger and more sombre than Wadebridge. Beams of sunlight penetrate the bomb-damaged roof, playing upon the remarkably clean Mogul. It is framed by roof girders, support columns and two engines – another class U on the left and the protruding smokebox of LBSCR class C2X No. 32549.

Plate 183 (*opposite, below*): At Shepton Mallet, a final tribute to the S&D and BR, featuring 2–10–0 class 9F No. 92001, second of its class, bearing down with a train to Bournemouth. This heaviest of BR classes can be overpowering if photographed too close. After careful setting of Depth of Field, an old wooden sign was introduced, relegating the train to the middle-distance. Framing is completed by a tall LSWR signal, two black huts, a goods siding and the far hillside with white house. The cut-out letters imply compulsory line-crossing!

Plate 184: On a 'cold' siding by Fratton MPD, a final tribute to the LBSCR, featuring 0–6–0 class E1 tank No. 32694, formerly No. 94 *Shorwell*. This low-perspective bow-shot uses strong side-light to bring out every rivet, lamp-iron and hose connection. The round-topped side-tanks are unmistakably 'Brighton'. This was William Stroudley's first class of goods engine of which seventy-two were built between 1874 and 1883, later reboilered by Marsh. To avoid unstable 'duality', the bold outline of the engine is offset to the left. 'Soft' framing is then provided by the LSWR signal-box, a glimpse of house-tops and some glorious tones of sky colour. It is an unusual portrait, but not one to be attempted on running lines. Personal safety is paramount in railway photography.

A wealth of Southern steam did once abound,
When trains in Southern green were all around;
Stately signals, red and yellow,
Signal-boxes, cream and mellow,
Great and simple station settings could be found.

A wealth of Southern railwaymen once served,
In office, cab and lineside haunts reserved
For driving, selling, planning,
Fitting, checking and maintaining;
Their cheerful Southern spirit is preserved.

(Author)

Index of Locomotive Classes and Named Trains

Numbers in right-hand columns refer to Plate numbers

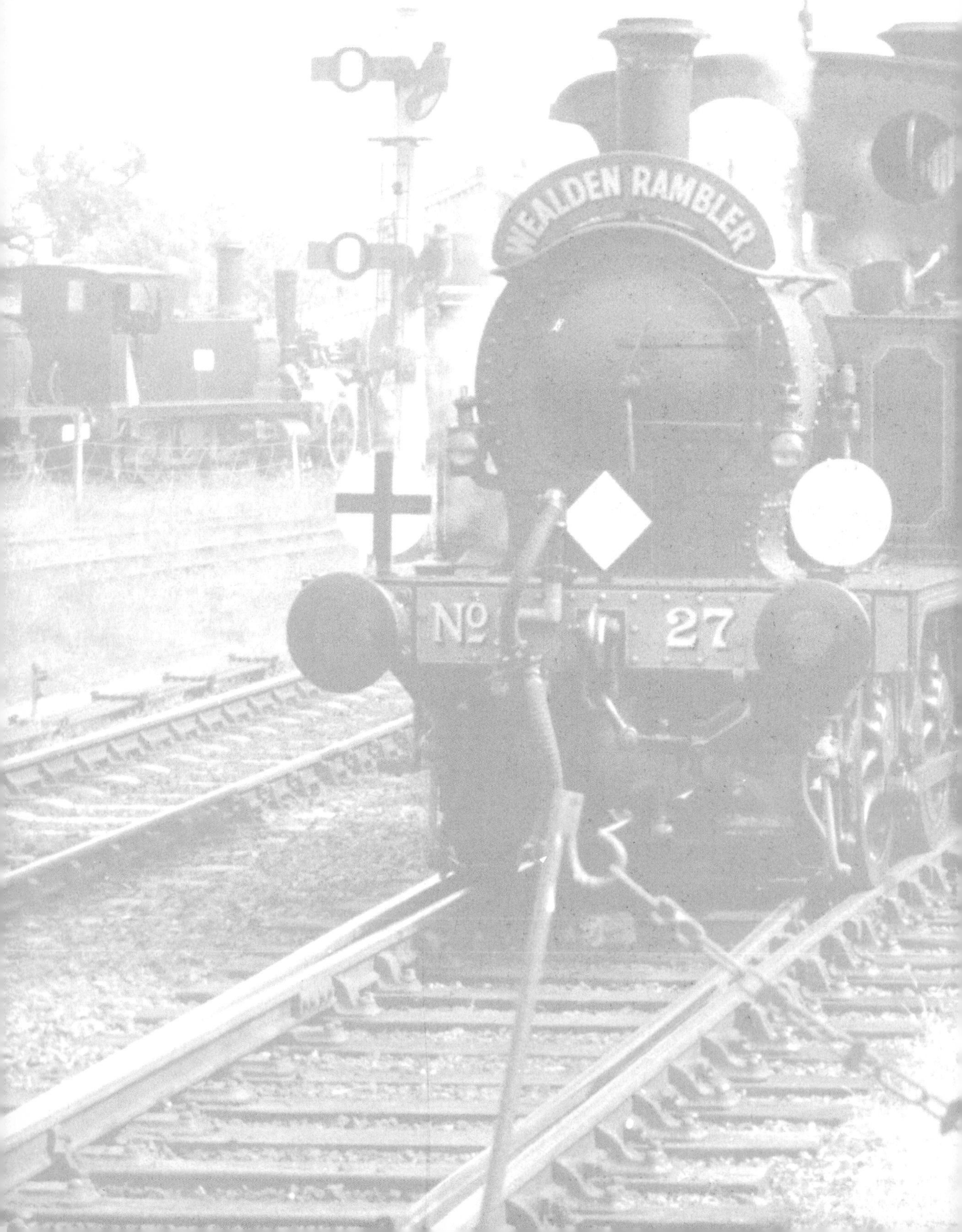
WEALDEN RAMBLER
No 27